ANTHROPOLOGY OF RELIGION

THE BASICS

D0706413

Anthropology of Religion: The Basics is an accessible and engaging introductory text organized around key issues that all anthropologists of religion face. This book uses a wide range of historical and ethnographic examples to address not only what is studied by anthropologists of religion, but how such studies are approached. It addresses such questions as:

- How do human agents interact with gods and spirits?
- What is the nature of doing religious ethnography?
- Can the immaterial be embodied in the body, language and material objects?
- What is the role of ritual, time, and place in religion?
- Why is charisma important for religious movements?
- How do global processes interact with religions?

With international case studies from a range of religious traditions, suggestions for further reading, and inventive reflection boxes, *Anthropology of Religion: The Basics* is an essential read for students approaching the subject for the first time.

James S. Bielo is a Lecturer in the Department of Anthropology at Miami University.

THE BASICS

ANTHROPOLOGY OF RELIGION

THE BASICS

James S. Bielo

Routledge
Taylor & Francis Group

LONDON AND NEW YORK

First published 2015
by Routledge
2 Park Square, Milton Park, Abingdon, Oxon OX14 4RN

and by Routledge
711 Third Avenue, New York, NY 10017

Routledge is an imprint of the Taylor & Francis Group, an informa business

British Library Cataloguing in Publication Data
A catalogue record for this book is available from the British Library

Library of Congress Cataloging in Publication Data
Bielo, James S.
Anthropology of religion : the basics / James Bielo.
pages cm. -- (The basics)
1. Anthropology of religion. I. Title.
GN470.B488 2015
306.6--dc23
2014031921

ISBN: 978-0-415-73124-9 (hbk)
ISBN: 978-0-415-73125-6 (pbk)
ISBN: 978-1-315-72840-7 (ebk)

Typeset in Bembo
by Taylor & Francis Books

CONTENTS

TABLES

PREFACE
READ ME FIRST (A NOTE TO STUDENTS AND INSTRUCTORS)

The most impactful course of my undergraduate career was "Anthropology of Religion." I was a student at Radford University in southwestern Virginia; spring semester, second year. At the time, studying religion was one among many interests of mine and not necessarily foremost on the list. Having grown up in a culturally Protestant region, and not an especially pious or intellectually curious household, I had very little understanding of American religious history and even less about global religious difference. In the small coastal county where I came of age (Lancaster, Virginia), religious pluralism more or less amounted to Baptists, Methodists, and Episcopalians. But as it often goes, I enrolled in the course because of the professor. In a previous course with Dr. Melinda Wagner, "Appalachian Cultures," I had learned a lot and liked her style. Most of all, her passion for ethnography and anthropology was magnetic.

Many of the course details and class experiences escape me now (why didn't I keep that syllabus!?!), but I do remember a bit. The course was divided in two halves. The first half was a survey of theory in the anthropology of religion; what most would call "classic" or "foundational" contributions to the field. We read essays from Edward Tylor, Emile Durkheim, Max Weber, Bronislaw Malinowski, E.E. Evans-Pritchard, Victor Turner, Clifford Geertz, and Roy Rappaport, among others. (Those names may not mean much to you now, but that will change as you work through this book.) I have a distinct memory of the exam day that concluded this half of the course; several hand-written pages of white notebook paper, filled front and back, comparing different theoretical frameworks. Dr. Wagner let me stay a few extra minutes to finish up; my right hand aching from the scribbling. Not sure if that sounds exciting to you, but for a 19-year-old young man with no exposure to a life of the mind, grappling with some of anthropology's seminal thinkers was something more than thrilling.

The second half of the course was devoted to a shared class project: the anthropology of apocalyptic communities. Each student chose a case study to research. Somehow, I selected Zoroastrianism and spent eight weeks immersed in a religious tradition I had never heard of before. There were about 15 students in the class, and during the final week of the semester we gave oral presentations on our respective projects. The region I grew up in was much more "golden rule Christianity" than "hell-fire-n-brimstone," so an ethnographic exploration of how different religions construe "the End of Days" was also a revelation.

Ultimately, the course was far greater than the sum of its parts. It planted deeply in me a sense of wanting to discover religious worlds, and a commitment that anthropology was a fantastic way to do that. Dr. Wagner, as John Steinbeck once wrote of the great artists we call teachers, "catalyzed a burning desire to know. Under their influence, the horizons sprung wide and fear went away and the unknown became knowable. But most important of all, the truth, that dangerous stuff, became beautiful and very precious" (1966 [2002]: 142).

After that spring semester, I stuck with the anthropology of religion. For my course in ethnographic methods during my final year at Radford, I spent the semester doing fieldwork with a small black Baptist congregation a few miles away from campus. I then headed to Michigan State University to study with Dr. Fredric Roberts. Like Melinda, Fred is a die-hard ethnographer and he mentored me for six years through a dissertation on American evangelical Bible study groups. (That's another story! (Bielo 2009)) During the

Bible study fieldwork I discovered a movement of cultural change stirring among evangelicals, and spent over three years studying the Emerging Church movement (Bielo 2011). As I write this, I am nearly three years into another ethnographic project, trying to understand how a team of creationist artists will design a biblical theme park (Bielo 2013).

After my years at Michigan State I began teaching at Miami University, in the small college town of Oxford, Ohio. Being at Miami has afforded me the opportunity to teach a broad range of courses, most of which are not squarely within my research focus. Thankfully, I have also been able to teach my first love: the anthropology of religion. That burning desire to know catalyzed by Melinda Wagner is as vibrant now as it was then, if not more so. I am continually fascinated by my ethnographic work with American evangelicals, as well as with broader questions of global religious diversity and the role of religion in our most pressing public debates and controversies. Religion is ever puzzling because it can be the source of ebullient joy and deadly violence, social solidarity and community unrest, lifelong existential struggle and lifelong commitment. Studying religion anthropologically has always struck me as an excellent way to understand not only particular religions, but also to understand something basic about the human condition.

A PROBLEM-ORIENTED APPROACH

Anthropology of Religion: The Basics emerges from my experiences becoming a professional anthropologist, doing ethnography with religious communities, and teaching the anthropology of religion. For the latter, it has been a struggle to find an introductory text that works well for the course structure and anthropological materials that I use. Please don't read me wrong. There are several very good "Anthropology of Religion" textbooks available: for example, John Bowen's *Religions in Practice* (2004) is a great resource and Morton Klass' *Ordered Universes* (1995) is as wonderfully provocative now as it was when first published. However, most of these textbooks are oriented around comparative topics in the study of religion. That is, they discuss case studies and theories that address an individual area of interest that anthropologists have studied cross-culturally. For example, individual chapters in these texts focus on topics like magic, witchcraft, shamanism, myth, ritual, religion and violence, religion and the senses, pilgrimage, healing, secularism, religious language, new religious movements, and so on. This book is different.

I have organized the book according to different research problems. By "problem" I mean a foundational source of inquiry. Problems are not reducible to particular topics or areas of interest. Rather, they are the grounding, the root, the underlying source of the research questions we ask. Research problems are inherently productive; they are the wellspring from which any given question or topic comes. Each of the problems we address in the chapters to follow have been pivotal for the anthropology of religion's liveliest debates and most enduring questions. Research problems are not like jigsaw puzzles you solve once and for all. They are more like steady churning engines, keeping the anthropology of religion in motion by continually producing new research questions to consider.

The six chapters in this book introduce and elaborate particular problems. Chapter 1 addresses our organizing category, "religion": why anthropologists define this term differently, critiques of the category, and the relationship of "religion" with a companion category, "the secular." Chapter 2 shifts the focus to a methodological problem: how to do the ethnography of religion. This chapter engages issues of ethics, fieldwork dynamics, and epistemology (how we know what we know). Chapter 3 addresses the problem of religious mediation: how individuals and communities use visible, material, and visceral resources to engage the immateriality of religion. We focus on three channels of mediation: bodies, words, and things. Chapter 4 explores the problem of religious world-making—that is, the ways in which religion provides a reality that adherents live within. Here, our discussion focuses on two axes of orientation: time and place. Chapter 5 examines the problem of religious authority: how social relations and institutions are grounded in trust, legitimacy, and power. In this chapter, a discussion of the social locations of religious authority leads into how religious authority exists in dynamic interaction with other cultural sources of authority (e.g., science). Finally, Chapter 6 takes on the problem of religious globalization. How do religious worlds interact with global and transnational processes?

Of course, there are other problems still to pursue. For example, there is the problem of agency (a chapter I originally planned to write but did not in order to keep the book an ideal length for classroom use). How do religious worlds attribute the capacity and power to act, think, and affect everyday life to both human and non-human actors? Or, we might consider the problem of religious pluralism: how multiple religious traditions co-exist, cooperatively and contentiously, in the same social context. Lucky for both of us, the goal of this book is not to be exhaustive. The goal is to equip you with intellectual tools that will enable you to decipher any research problem and investigate any research question. (For instructors, you might consider an assignment possibility here: ask students to outline an additional research problem using these chapters as a model.)

This book is also organized by an ethnographic imperative. Each chapter uses a diverse range of case studies to illustrate the research problem and questions being discussed. Almost without exception, the examples presented are studies of religion that emerge from in-depth fieldwork. For cultural and linguistic anthropologists, ethnography is the primary method for creating knowledge and the primary grounding for making scholarly claims. Ethnography is also effectively used by sociologists and religious studies scholars. As a result, we have an extraordinary ethnographic record of human religiosity and I hope this book conveys some of that richness.

This ethnographic imperative also fuels the reflection boxes that conclude most major sections in the chapters. These boxes are decidedly not passive reviews of the material presented in the section. Every reflection box is an invitation to expand on the work presented by applying concepts to examples of religion in practice. If you are conducting original research or fieldwork for your course, the reflection boxes encourage you to think of the issues being presented in light of your own project. Otherwise, the boxes direct you to an online resource or documentary film for analysis. You should be able to locate each film using your departmental, university, or community library (and, in several cases, entire films are viewable on YouTube). For instructors, I encourage you to consider using the reflection boxes for multiple purposes. They can be used as the basis for an in-class exercise, out-of-class assignment, or extra credit.

The ethnographic imperative is, in part, what distinguishes an anthropological approach to studying religion. Other forms of knowledge are necessary and useful, such as demographic statistics, histories, biographies, and close readings of religious texts. But, all of these remain incomplete without the anthropological focus on religion as practiced, embodied, and lived. The anthropological study of religion is also distinctive because anthropology is distinctive from other disciplines. For example, anthropologists of religion maintain the broader disciplinary commitments to cultural relativism, holistic analysis, comparative thinking, and abduction (i.e., persistently oscillating between empirical data and general theory). While distinctive, the anthropology of religion has never been disengaged from or completely unlike other approaches to the study of religion. Throughout the course of this book, we will highlight many points of contact between anthropology, religious studies, sociology, history, and philosophy.

THE BASICS

It is a bit ironic that I agreed to write this book. The reason is that I tend to shy away from using introductory texts in all of my courses. Mostly, I use at least one book-length ethnography as the central text(s) and design compilations of published essays as a course reader. Most textbooks have a few tendencies that I find unhelpful. More often than not, they read in an overly pedantic way, prioritize breadth of knowledge over any depth, fail to direct students in pursuing original analyses, and (implicitly or explicitly) claim an exhaustive account of the subject material presented. (Granted, this is my bias and there are certainly exceptions.)

However, I was immediately attracted by the premise of Routledge's "The Basics" series. I greatly appreciate the idea of an introductory text (versus the typical textbook/door stopper) that presents some essential elements of a field as a springboard for students to explore further on their own. Moreover, there is an unceasing need for all of us to continually practice the basics in our fields of expertise. Like the world-class footballer who never stops working on skills like passing and controlling the ball, the anthropologist of religion has basic sensibilities to keep sharp. Becoming and staying as sharp as possible: that is the spirit of this book.

I envision *Anthropology of Religion: The Basics* as an ideal companion volume. For instructors, I recommend using the book in conjunction with either a more traditional textbook, a series of ethnographic readings, or one of the many edited volumes designed specifically for anthropology of religion courses. In terms of course structure, the six chapters can serve as the initial reading for six course units (on a semester schedule, this amounts to roughly two weeks per unit). Naturally, if you already have an approach for your course honed and polished, this book can work equally well as required supplemental reading (again, highlighting the reflection boxes for multiple course purposes).

I wrote this book over a two-year period, between early 2013 and late 2014. During that time, my thinking and writing has benefitted from the keen and curious intellects of both colleagues and students. Among the former, I want to recognize the contributions and influence of a few individuals (with apologies to many others who deserve to be named): John Cinnamon, Rory Johnson, Jeb Card, Homayun Sidky, Mark Peterson, Leighton Peterson, Jon Bialecki, Naomi Haynes, Tom Boylston, Eric Hoenes, Omri Elisha, Brian Howell, Rebekka King, Hillary Kaell, Jackie Feldman, Andy Blanton, Catherine Wanner, Simon Coleman, Matthew Engelke, Joel Robbins, Susan Harding, Tanya Luhrmann, Pamela Klassen, Don Seeman, Joe Webster, Bill Girard, Matt Tomlinson, Fred Klaits, John Jackson, Greg Starrett, Vincent Wimbush, John Schmalzbauer, Gerardo Marti, Kathryn Lofton, Natalia Suit, and (in perpetuity and then some) Melinda Wagner and Fred Roberts. Additionally, anonymous reviewers of the book proposal and manuscript offered insightful readings at several junctures.

I owe a special thank you to a small group of students at Miami University. These students read early chapter drafts and provided incisive reviews, all of which helped shape the final manuscript. With all the gratitude I can muster, thanks to: Emily Crane, Michele Bailey, Monica Neff, Allison Burko, and the spring 2014 cohort of "ATH403: Anthropology of Religion" (Caroline Johnson, Samantha Cardarelli, Amber Scott, Meghan Mullins, Kate Hewig, Matt Finch, Brad Phillip, Kaitlyn Hunter, Gabriella Uli, Evan Brown, Thomas Bollow, Mary Ann Nueva, Qili Guo, and Alicia Norrod.)

I learned a great deal writing this book and had a lot of fun working with the material. I hope readers will benefit equally as much!

WHAT IS "RELIGION"?

Today's anthropology of religion explores a wonderfully diverse range of phenomena. We chase and immerse ourselves in everything from the study of globalized religions (like Christianity and Islam) to sectarian movements, indigenous traditions, irreligious and anti-religious groups. To help orient our study of such groups and movements we consider an equally complex set of comparative topics. A partial listing includes magic, witchcraft, ritual, myth, shamanism, sorcery, divination, conversion, spirit possession, healing, prayer, prophecy, pilgrimage, humanitarian outreach, socio-political activism, missionization, religious change, and inter-religious dialogue.

What brings such a diverse collection together? What unites them all as expressions of the same category: "religion"? After all, religion as a human phenomenon cannot be reduced to any particular cultural expression or social form. So, then, what is religion?

This chapter's title poses a seemingly simple question. Answering that question is a different story entirely. For readers seeking a definitive, succinct answer, please accept my apologies upfront. No such answer is coming. But, my bet and my hope is that by the end of this chapter you will appreciate why a definitive, succinct answer would be unhelpful and misleading. The goal of this chapter is to help you critically reflect on the category "religion": what its nature might be, why different scholars at different times have advocated different ideas about this, and what value (if any) the category offers. We begin by comparing a series of anthropological definitions. Along the way, we ask what each teaches us about the problem of defining "religion."

DEFINING IS THEORIZING

Why begin with definitions? It is not so we can pin down a final, triumphant understanding of the anthropology of religion's organizing category. It is also not because this is a requisite discussion, an exercise we absolutely must do. (As we'll see below, some scholars argue that any attempt to secure a unifying definition is a fool's errand.) We begin with definitions because how a scholar defines religion reveals important insights about their basic assumptions and commitments in the study of religion. In short, definitions are clues to theoretical orientation.

Why does theory matter so much? Ultimately, theoretical orientation is instrumental in deciding what to study, what research questions matter most, what counts as data, how to collect data, how to analyze data, and how to represent what was studied. Different anthropologists at different points in the discipline's history have favored certain orientations over others. Some have asked "What are the human origins of religion?" while others have asked "What does religion do for individuals and for societies?" "How do people use religion in everyday life?" "What is the psychological and emotional substance of religious experience?" "How does religion shape, and how is it shaped by, other social institutions?" or "What is unique about religion as a human phenomenon?" These divergent questions reflect different theoretical orientations. Comparing definitions is a good way to begin to grasp the differences and why they matter.

In the Preface we suggested that an anthropological approach to religion overlaps with, but is also distinct from, other social science and humanities disciplines. Ideally, an anthropological approach would do several things. It would be grounded in empirical research, primarily ethnographic and archival. It would be comparative, so that it is cross-culturally useful. It would not be geared toward creating hierarchies or separating "good" from "bad" religion. And, it would enhance broader anthropological aims like holism and cultural relativism. As we begin comparing definitions, ask how well each definition satisfies these ideals.

Below, we compare nine definitions. Our goal is not to decide which definition is ultimately correct, and it is not so we can intervene with our own final, triumphant definition. We follow the lead of Thomas Tweed, an historian and ethnographer of religion, who writes that definitions should be approached as "only more or less useful" (2006: 34). All of these definitions have something to teach us. This posture is helpful for two reasons. First, comparing definitions in this way is intellectually generous: it asks what is valuable about any given approach to the study of religion. Second, this posture encourages self-reflection: we are poised to better understand our own commitments when we consider why we are attracted to some definitions and not others, why we find some productive and others not.

A PRIMER

To begin, it is useful to observe that some of the most influential thinkers in the study of religion did not actually offer operational definitions. Rather, they articulated a theoretical sensibility, a way of thinking about religion. Consider three classic examples: Karl Marx, Sigmund Freud, and Max Weber.

Karl Marx (1818–83), a philosopher and early sociologist famous for his critique of industrial capitalism, did not produce a large volume of work about religion. His influence far outstrips the amount of words he penned (see Raines 2002 for a selection of these writings). But, in 1844 he published this widely cited statement in an essay, "Critique of Hegel's 'Philosophy of Right'":

> Man makes religion, religion does not make Man ... Man is the world of Man, the state, society. This state, this society, produce religion, a reversed world consciousness, because they are a reversed world. Religion is the general theory of that world, its encyclopedic compendium, its logic in popular form, its enthusiasm, its moral sanction, its universal ground for consolation and justification. It is the fantastic realization of the human essence because the human essence has no true reality ... [Religion] is the opium of the people.

From this, two ideas about the nature of religion linger for many anthropologists. First, his opening statement, "Man makes religion," is both theological and sociological. Marx was arguing against the idea that humans are somehow naturally religious and that religious systems have any origin other than human society. Religion is a human product. Second, Marx understood religion as a form of false consciousness, "a reversed world consciousness," that distracts people from this-worldly problems (poverty, for example). Religion is a veil, blinding people to life's pressing realities. Perhaps his most enduring phrase, "the opium of the people," conveys his normative stance: religion is a drug. All this resonates with Marx's broader framework of cultural and economic critique: industrial capitalism brutalizes workers and workers do not revolt because they remain blind to the conditions of their domination. Marx wanted to pull the curtain back, to reveal those brutal conditions. Naming religion as part of modern society's false consciousness was part of this broader critique.

Sigmund Freud (1856–1939), one of psychology's most recognizable figures, also viewed religion in negative terms. Unlike Marx, Freud did write a lot about religion. Beginning with a short essay in 1907, "Obsessive Actions and Religious Practices," and continuing in three books—*Totem and Taboo* (1913), *The Future of an Illusion* (1927), and *Moses and Monotheism* (1937)—Freud presented religion as a kind of neurotic behavior and as a grand illusion. Religion lingers in modern life because it satisfies a base psychological need to feel protected from fears (death, for example). Like Marx, Freud's approach was part of a larger project: psychoanalysis as an attempt to rid people of the psychological baggage that restricted their development into healthy mature adulthood. Naming religion as a dysfunctional hurdle to get over was part of this broader critique.

Max Weber (1864–1920), an extremely influential German sociologist, offers a less skewed posture for the study of religion. Weber's most extensive case study of modern religion, *The Protestant Ethic and the "Spirit" of Capitalism*, was first published in 1905 (translated into English in 1930). This book explores how theology, morality, labor, social organization, and economic change are deeply entangled. Weber, a more sophisticated analyst of religion than Marx or Freud, also evades a definition. He wrote in a 1922 essay:

> Definition can be attempted, if at all, only at the conclusion of the study. The essence of religion is not even our concern, as we make it our task to study the conditions and effects of a particular type of social behavior. The external courses of religious behaviors are so diverse that an understanding of this behavior can only be achieved from the viewpoint of the subjective experiences, ideas, and purposes of the individuals concerned—in short, from the viewpoint of the religious behavior's "meaning."

Weber makes some revealing statements here. First, he shifts the focus from "essence" to "conditions and effects." While some scholars have persisted in trying to articulate what the essence of religion is, others have followed Weber's lead in exploring the social sources and social consequences of religion. Second, Weber prioritizes "subjective experiences, ideas, and purposes," or simply, the "meaning" of religion to religious adherents themselves. This suggests that scholars can and should seek to understand the inner life of religious people.

Marx, Freud, and Weber do not provide local (that is, culturally specific) or universal definitions of "religion." What they do is articulate a sensibility, an approach, a way of studying religion. They are instructive for our analysis below because they begin to demonstrate how approach matters. Marx and Freud employ a hermeneutics of suspicion, which means they interpret religion as obscuring something more fundamental to human reality. For them, it is the scholar's duty to see beyond religion's mystifications and identify the more fundamental force (for Marx, it was economic conflict; for Freud, psychic turmoil). Weber was different. He was committed to contextualizing religion in the lived social world ("conditions and effects"), while also wanting to understand religion on its own terms ("meaning"). As we compare definitions, ask what kind of posture toward religion is being suggested. I have divided the nine definitions into two sets. The first four we'll call "Foundational" because they were articulated early in anthropology's development as a discipline and because they established certain terms of debate that still thrive.

FOUNDATIONAL DEFINITIONS

We begin with two "armchair" scholars, early contributors to what the scope of anthropological inquiry might be: an Englishman E.B. Tylor (1832–1917) and a Scot, James Frazer (1854–1941).

Tylor and Frazer are often called armchair anthropologists because their writings relied on others' reports (explorers and missionaries, for example), not their own ethnographic fieldwork.

In his 1871 volume *Religion in Primitive Culture*, Tylor penned what might be the first modern anthropological definition of religion. He aimed for simplicity, writing that all human religion is united by "belief in spiritual beings." This simplicity was not incidental. He sought a common thread to connect Christianity's monotheism and the animism of tribal societies recorded throughout his collection of archeological, missionary, and traveler accounts. Animism was a term Tylor made popular, meaning the attribution of spiritual will (or essence) to non-human entities (e.g., animals or features of the natural world). Tylor wanted a common thread in order to support his theory of cultural evolutionism: all human societies were biologically similar but existed in different stages of a hierarchical progression. He saw the study of animism as the study of religious origins. "Belief in spiritual beings" was what linked the earliest form of religion to its evolutionary descendants of polytheism and monotheism.

Despite this theoretical agenda, which no modern anthropologist would support, Tylor articulated two commitments that have lingered in the anthropology of religion: a focus on belief and on the supernatural. By focusing on belief, Tylor focused on the inner psychological life of religious actors, ideas about the nature of life, and explanations for why things are the way they are. By focusing on the supernatural, Tylor focused on agencies different from ordinary, living human beings. Both of these commitments have received substantial criticism as the basis for cross-cultural theorizing, but they continue to persist as touchstones in the study of religion.

Tylor was a major inspiration for Frazer's work, *The Golden Bough: A Study in Magic and Religion* (1890). Like *Religion in Primitive Culture*, this was a massive project of comparative ethnology. Frazer defines religion as "a propitiation or conciliation of powers superior to man which are believed to direct and control the course of nature and of human life." Frazer retains the focus on belief and the supernatural ("powers superior to man"), but adds his own lingering contribution: religion is centrally concerned with establishing order ("direct and control the course of nature and of human life").

Frazer was also committed to cultural evolutionism and *The Golden Bough* intended to demonstrate how human societies progress through three systems that explain life's orderliness: magic, religion, and science. For Frazer, science was the pinnacle of human advancement and religion a vestige of our pre-modern past. Despite this agenda, Frazer introduced substantial nuance to the study of religion. For example, he elaborated the distinction between sympathetic and contagious magic. These two methods operate according to different logics: sympathetic magic works by a rule of imitation ✓ (think: the scene in the 1984 film *Indiana Jones and the Temple of Doom* when the Maharaja stabs the doll of Indy) whereas contagious magic works by a rule of unbreakable physical connection (think: the use of someone's hair, skin, or fingernails to cast a protective or harmful spell). Scholars still use this distinction to discuss how different kinds of magic work to establish order.

Anthropologists have always integrated the work of other social scientists, natural scientists, philosophers, and artists into our thinking. The study of religion is no exception. The next two definitions come respectively from an American psychologist, William James (1842–1910), and a French sociologist, Emile Durkheim (1858–1917).

At the turn of the 20th century, William James was an international academic celebrity. In 1901 and 1902 he delivered a series of lectures at the University of Edinburgh, subsequently published as *The Varieties of Religious Experience: A Study in Human Nature* (1902). The book compares a wide range of literary, historical, psychological, and ethnological examples of human religiosity. James defines religion as "the feelings, acts, and experiences of individual men in their ✓ solitude, so far as they apprehend themselves to stand in relation to whatever they may consider the divine."

James' work was a critique of both the religious and scientific establishments. He wanted to broaden the scope of what being religious meant beyond institutional and organizational confines, whence the focus on "individual men in their solitude." And, he wanted to broaden the scope of claims to truth beyond scientific proofs. All of this was part of James' larger project of developing a pragmatist philosophy. Pragmatism is a complicated system, but *The Varieties* captures one of its core commitments: truth should be gauged by usefulness. For James, religious experience was true and real because it provoked real people to do real things in the real world, even if those experiences could not be measured via natural science. This focus on "experience" has proved quite durable for anthropologists of religion. Rather than key in on social structures or functions (think: Weber's "conditions and effects"), James spotlighted the visceral, sensorial, emotional, and psychological real-ness of religious experience for individuals.

Emile Durkheim was also an academic luminary when he published his last major book, *The Elementary Forms of Religious Life* (1912). Read most any history of the social sciences and you will find Durkheim named as a founder of sociology (usually alongside Karl Marx and Max Weber). In *The Elementary Forms* Durkheim defined religion as "a unified set of beliefs and practices relative to sacred things, that is to say, things set apart and forbidden—beliefs and practices which unite one single moral community called a Church, all those who adhere to them." Durkheim adds a focus on "practices" to the familiar "beliefs," and, not surprisingly for a sociologist, emphasizes human collectivity ("moral community"). Throughout *The Elementary Forms*, he elevates practices (in particular, group rituals) as more integral than beliefs for sustaining the social project of moral community.

Perhaps most important, Durkheim contributes the notion of the sacred to the study of religion. At its core the sacred is about a division: "things set apart and forbidden" as wholly distinct from aspects of society not deemed special for sustaining moral community (what he called "the profane"). Understanding religion, then, is not about identifying supernatural forces or spirits; it is about identifying what a society reveres. The sacred is what is worshipped, and what is worshipped is the religious. For Durkheim, this all demonstrated a crucial piece of his broader project: to explain how human societies maintain cohesion, mutuality, and belonging—i.e., moral community. In functionalist terms, religion was simply a very powerful institution to achieve this basic social mandate.

So, what is religion? Four scholars, each influential in their own right, define the term differently. At this point, I hope you are tracking with two observations. First, each definition contributes something to the big tent we call the anthropology of religion. Second, each definition reflects a commitment to a broader scholarly project: Tylor and Frazer's cultural evolutionism, James' pragmatism, and Durkheim's functionalism. From here, we continue our analysis with five, more contemporary, anthropological definitions.

CONTEMPORARY ELABORATIONS

In the decades following the work of Tylor, Frazer, James, and Durkheim, anthropology came into its own as a discipline. Led by Franz Boas in the United States and Bronislaw Malinowski in England, anthropology became synonymous with long-term, ethnographic fieldwork. As a result, anthropologists spent considerably more time doing empirical work with religious communities. In turn, attempts to theorize religion emerged more directly from research findings (that is, the messy, complicated stuff of human religiosity). For example, Paul Radin (1883–1959), a student of Boas, used his fieldwork among different American Indian tribes to write *Primitive Religion: Its Nature and Origin* (1937). Radin defines religion in "two parts":

> The first an easily definable, if not precisely specific feeling; and the second certain specific acts, customs, beliefs, and conceptions associated with this feeling. The belief most inextricably connected with the specific feeling is a belief in spirits outside of man, conceived of as more powerful than man and as controlling all those elements in life upon which he lays most stress.
>
> (3)

Radin's definition reveals three things. First, similar to William James, Radin uses emotion as a baseline to identify religion. Second, à la Tylor, belief is elevated over ritual ("acts, customs"). Third, again à la Tylor, he makes the existence of non-human agencies ("spirits") integral to religion, invoking the category of the supernatural. And, he conceives these agencies to be forcefully involved in human affairs, invoking a this-world/other-world relationship.

A Canadian anthropologist, Anthony F.C. Wallace (1923–), also wrote an influential volume, *Religion: An Anthropological View* (1966). Wallace is a prolific ethnographer, historian, and theorist (see Chapter 5 for more on Wallace, namely his theory of revitalization movements). In his 1966 volume Wallace defines religion as, "a set of rituals, rationalized by myth, which mobilizes supernatural powers for the purpose of achieving or preventing transformations of state in man and nature" (107). He then elaborated on the "minimal categories of behavior" that constituted "the substance of religion itself":

> Although almost any behavior can be invested with a religious meaning, there seems to be a finite number—about 13—of behavior categories, most of which are, in any religious system, combined into a pattern that is conventionally assigned the title "religion."
>
> (52)

He went on to name the 13: prayer, music, physiological exercise, exhortation, reciting the code, simulation, *mana*, taboo, feasts, sacrifice, congregation, inspiration, and symbolism. For Wallace, religion was made of a combination between select ritual practices and the effects of those practices on social and natural conditions ("achieving or preventing transformations"). Note that he prioritizes behavior (ritual practices) and social organization (institutions) to establish "the substance of religion," not the Weberian focus on investing behavior with meaning. And, like Frazer, James, and Radin, Wallace emphasizes the practical nature of religion—people use it to get things done.

Our next definition is perhaps the most widely cited in the set, and comes from Clifford Geertz (1926–2006). Geertz is a central figure in the history of anthropology, primarily because he outlined the theoretical approach of interpretive anthropology. Interpretive anthropology prioritizes humans as meaning-makers and producer-consumers of public symbols. The anthropologist's job is to decode the socially shared meanings communicated through symbolic systems. In a 1966 essay, "Religion as a Cultural System," Geertz defines religion in a way consistent with that broader theoretical orientation:

> a system of symbols which acts to establish powerful, pervasive, and long-lasting moods and motivations in men by formulating conceptions of a general order of existence and clothing these conceptions with such an aura of factuality that the moods and motivations seem uniquely realistic.
>
> (4)

At the heart of Geertz's definition are symbols, "any object, act, event, quality, or relation which serves as a vehicle for a conception," integrated as a system. Geertz revives Frazer's interest in religion as a means to establish orderliness ("conceptions of a general order of existence"). And, Geertz picks up James' thread of emphasizing the emotive aspect of religion ("long-lasting moods and motivations").

In a smart, pithy book, *Ordered Universes: Approaches to the Anthropology of Religion* (1995), Morton Klass (1927–2001) reviewed existing definitions in order to formulate his own, one that would eliminate ethnocentric baggage. He viewed most key concepts in the anthropology of religion as ethnocentric because they made certain religious traditions central while marginalizing others. For example, making "supernatural" definitive is inherently biased toward theistic religions. Ultimately, he settled on this definition:

> Religion in a given society will be that instituted process of interaction among the members of that society—and between them and the universe at large as they conceive it to be constituted—which provides them with meaning, coherence, direction, unity easement, and whatever degree of control over events they perceive as possible.

(38)

Klass manages to integrate multiple aspects: the definition has one foot in the immanently social ("interaction among the members of that society") and one in the transcendent ("the universe at large"). It recalls Durkheim ("meaning, coherence, direction, unity easement") and Frazer ("control over events").

Our final definition comes from Scott Atran (1952–) and his book, *In Gods We Trust: The Evolutionary Landscape of Religion* (2002):

> Religion is a community's costly and hard-to-fake commitment to a counterfactual and counterintuitive world of supernatural agents who master people's existential activities, such as death and deception.

Atran approaches religion from the standpoint of biological evolution. In this theoretical orientation, religion is a cognitive by-product of the human evolutionary process. It has stuck around through millions of years because it fosters successful adaptation. This hard-wired view of religion helps explain terms like "costly," "hard-to-fake," "counterfactual," and "counterintuitive." Like Tylor's "belief in spiritual beings," Atran articulates a strictly cognitive view of religion: it exists as a mental phenomenon.

There are at least two important observations to make from comparing these nine definitions. First, let's recall our pool of definitions (Table 1.1).

Table 1.1 Nine definitions of "religion"

Author	Date	Definition
Tylor	1871	Belief in spiritual beings
Frazer	1890	A propitiation or conciliation of powers superior to man which are believed to direct and control the course of nature and of human life
James	1902	The feelings, acts, and experiences of individual men in their solitude, so far as they apprehend themselves to stand in relation to whatever they may consider the divine
Durkheim	1912	A unified set of beliefs and practices relative to sacred things, that is to say, things set apart and forbidden—beliefs and practices which unite one single moral community called a Church, all those who adhere to them
Radin	1937	[Religion] consists of two parts: the first an easily definable, if not precisely specific feeling; and the second certain specific acts, customs, beliefs, and conceptions associated with this feeling. The belief most inextricably connected with the specific feeling is a belief in spirits outside of man, conceived of as more powerful than man and as controlling all those elements in life upon which he lays most stress
Wallace	1966	A set of rituals, rationalized by myth, which mobilizes supernatural powers for the purpose of achieving or preventing transformations of state in man and nature
Geertz	1966	A system of symbols which acts to establish powerful, pervasive, and long-lasting moods and motivations in men by formulating conceptions of a general order of existence and clothing these conceptions with such an aura of factuality that the moods and motivations seem uniquely realistic
Klass	1995	That instituted process of interaction among the members of that society—and between them and the universe at large as they conceive it to be constituted—which provides them with meaning, coherence, direction, unity easement, and whatever degree of control over events they perceive as possible
Atran	2002	A community's costly and hard-to-fake commitment to a counterfactual and counterintuitive world of supernatural agents who master people's existential activities, such as death and deception

The first observation is that these definitions present a range of aspects as instrumental for defining religion. Some highlight only one, as Tylor did with belief. Some highlight multiple aspects, as Durkheim does by calling attention to belief, practice, the sacred, and moral community. Some elevate the social over the individual; others, like James, elevate individual experience. Certain aspects re-appear in different guises. For example, Frazer, Durkheim, Geertz, and Klass all say in their own way that religion establishes order. No sample of definitions could completely exhaust the possible aspects in studying religion, but this sample names many of the usual suspects: belief, order, experience, the sacred, ritual practice, and symbolic meaning. (Note a conspicuous absence on this list: materiality. How might things—physical objects that are naturally occurring or made by humans—be used to define religion? Chapter 3 will help us think about this.)

A second observation is one we have made several times: definitions are clues to broader theoretical and/or normative commitments. We must understand Tylor and Frazer's definitions in light of their cultural evolutionism, Geertz's in relation to interpretive anthropology, and Atran's in relation to evolutionary anthropology. This link between definition and theory will not always be crystal clear, but I hope this exercise has demonstrated that there will be a link and it is your job, as a critical reader, to find it.

Of course, there are many worthwhile definitions of religion we did not mention. Our point was not to be exhaustive (a futile task in any case!), but to demonstrate the importance that definitional difference makes. We might conclude from this that defining religion is a no-win game and there's no sense playing it. But, what if we take a different tack? What if we presume that our most important terms are those that generate the most disagreement? Even if a silver bullet definition that is universally satisfying eludes us, which it will, we benefit from doing the work of analyzing why definitions are composed as they are.

Box 1.1 Defining "religion" is a high stakes game

In this section we saw how definitions of "religion" do more than simply define; they tell us what is being prioritized in the study of religion. If you are still getting comfortable with this idea, you might expand the comparative exercise. Collect three more anthropological definitions of religion (simply by using Google or through a library search engine).

- What aspects does each highlight (e.g., belief, ritual, morality, order)?
- What theoretical orientation(s) are reflected by each definition?
- If you're working with a class colleague, trade your three definitions with each other and do your own independent analysis. Meet up and compare your findings. Did you identify the same aspects? Did you use different terms to talk about similar phenomena? Did you identify similar theoretical orientations?

If you are comfortable with this definitional exercise, you can work with the following.

Defining religion is not merely an academic exercise, nor is it only of value and consequence for scholars. Nation-states are also in the game of defining "religion," and their conclusions have significant legal, political, and economic stakes. For example, in the United States obtaining legal status as a "church" carries several privileges, including: exemptions on property taxes and zoning ordinances; restrictions on how and when the IRS can conduct a tax audit; and, access to resources from the State Department's Office of Faith-Based Initiatives. A famous example of an organization seeking legal status as a church is Scientology (Urban 2011). L. Ron Hubbard, the founder of the Scientology movement, first incorporated a church in 1953 and the state of California was the first to grant Scientology tax exempt status as a "church" in 1957. However, from 1958 until 1993 the Church of Scientology and the IRS traded lawsuits debating whether Scientology should be recognized as a religious organization. Scientology prevailed. Still, as a movement with global ambitions, Scientology remains unrecognized as a religion in, among other places, Canada, Germany, Greece, Belgium, and France. On your own, or with class colleagues, explore the Church of Scientology website: www.scientology.org/.

- How does the movement represent itself as a religion?
- What aspects (e.g., belief, ritual) does the movement appeal to?

Less-publicized examples of claiming and challenging the legal rights of being a religion unfold regularly in the United States. On your own, or with class colleagues, examine a lawsuit filed by the non-profit organization American Atheists (*American Atheists v. Shulman, 2014*): atheists.org/legal/current/IRS. Their lawsuit seeks to eliminate the distinction made by the state of Kentucky and the IRS between "religious organizations" and other non-profits, which only grants religious organizations a tax exempt status.

- On what legal grounds do American Atheists make their challenge?
- How is American Atheists' philosophical critique of religion evidenced?
- What does this case suggest about the legal, political, and economic stakes of a nation-state defining "religion"?

CRITIQUES OF "RELIGION"

Any category that receives as much definitional attention as "religion" is bound to also receive critical attention. For some scholars, to critique is to sharpen a category for better use. For others, critique is about challenging a category's legitimacy. In this section we consider two anthropological critiques of "religion": skepticism about the term's cross-cultural validity, and challenges to the central role of belief. Through these examples, we reflect on why some scholars have turned a critical eye on "religion" and what contributions those criticisms make to ongoing comparative research.

QUESTIONING "RELIGION"

Recall Frazer's distinction among magic, religion, and science. Also, recall that Frazer was thinking as a cultural evolutionist. As systems of explanation, "religion" is positioned superior to "magic" and inferior to "science." One critique is that by continuing to use the term "religion" we perpetuate this hierarchy. Here, "religion" is considered inherently ethnocentric because it emerges from a system that values Western modernity above any alternative way of life.

E.E. Evans-Pritchard (1902–73) was an early critic of separating magic and religion as discrete categories. "E-P," as colleagues affectionately knew him, was a key figure in British social anthropology. A consummate ethnographer, his first long-term study was among the Azande of southern Sudan, from which he wrote his first book: *Witchcraft, Oracles, and Magic among the Azande* (1937). E-P was very much a social anthropologist, dedicated to explaining social structure and organization. But, he was also quite taken with the inner logics of Zande religious practice. In particular, he was enthralled with how witchcraft pervaded everyday life, "there is no niche or corner of Zande culture into which it does not twist itself" (18). He explained that witchcraft replaces a mechanism like coincidence, by providing a ready explanation for otherwise inexplicable forms of harm, failure, and misfortune. "We see that witchcraft has its own logic, its own rules of thought, and that these do not exclude natural causation. Belief in witchcraft is quite consistent with human responsibility and a rational appreciation of nature" (30). As an everyday explanatory system, Zande witchcraft works extremely well for its practitioners, no less so than any form of religion in other cultural settings.

E-P wrote against a strict religion–magic divide from the strength of his ethnographic fieldwork. A more ambitious theoretical critique came from one of his students, Talal Asad (1933–). In his book *Genealogies of Religion: Discipline and Reasons of Power in Christianity and Islam* (1993), Asad historicized the concept of religion and its role in anthropology. He traced the category's modern usage to post-Reformation Europe, where defining "religion" was a specifically Christian project geared toward demarcating religion from other social domains (e.g., politics). Asad argued that "there cannot be a universal definition of religion" (29) because all such definitions ultimately reflect the historical and ideological context of their production more than they do any objective phenomenon.

Asad carefully dissects Geertz's 1966 definition, using it to exemplify the inherent problems of positing a universal definition. For Asad, one problem has to do with properly recognizing the role of authority in religious life. By elevating cultural products like symbols to be the core of religion, Geertz ignores the social conditions and processes that produce, circulate and endow those products with authority. These conditions and processes are thoroughly relations of unequal power; only certain people have the ability to produce, circulate, and endow. (Consider the difference between analyzing the meaning of symbols and analyzing the institutional and ideological pathways by which those symbols get legitimized.) Asad's suspicion of religion as a valid category emerges from his theoretical commitment, to understand power relationships, inspired by post-colonial thinkers like Michel Foucault and Edward Said.

A Dutch anthropologist, Peter van der Veer, extends the critique that religion is an expression of Western colonialism. In his book *The Modern Spirit of Asia: The Spiritual and the Secular in China and India* (2014), van der Veer compares how Indian and Chinese officials managed the diverse traditions within their geo-political boundaries. He argues that becoming modern (that is, joining Western nations as part of a global elite) meant performing a division between the religious and the secular:

> It is imperialism that forces Indians and Chinese to interpret their traditions in terms of the category of religion and its opposition to the secular ... It is the imperial context that produces a remarkably similar trajectory which essentializes Hinduism, Buddhism, Islam, Christianity, Daoism, and even Confucianism into comparable entities, subjects of the new, secular discipline of comparative religion or science of religion.
>
> (145)

Here, the category of "religion" functions as a political device, a way of categorizing people that was familiar and acceptable to Western thinking. Indigenous systems that varied widely from one locale to another and melded quite freely were "essentialized." They were transformed into singular, nameable, and describable entities that were separable from other systems: Buddhists aren't Daoists who aren't Confucianists. For van der Veer, this political use of "religion" fostered the colonial imperative to manage the populace.

TROUBLES WITH BELIEF

Is religion a normative category saddled by ethnocentrism? Critics like Asad and van der Veer, who are sympathetic with this critique, challenge the cross-cultural validity of "religion" in order to improve anthropology. They are not just naysayers. They are trying to build better frameworks for understanding people and their socio-cultural worlds. This aim to improve has also fueled suspicions about "belief."

Critics target "belief" because it has played a prominent role in the anthropology of religion. Belief is used in definitions to characterize the nature of religion. Belief is used to differentiate one group from another: the religious and the non-religious have diverging beliefs; Hindus differ from Muslims and Jews and Sikhs and Buddhists and Christians by what beliefs they require. And, belief is said to under-write action: people do things—religious ritual, religious violence, religious charity—because of what beliefs they hold.

The first sustained dissection of "belief" came in a 1972 book by British anthropologist Rodney Needham (1923–2006), *Belief, Language, and Experience*. Needham implored that the term be abandoned. He argued that it lacked cross-cultural reliability; evident by the fact that the English term often lacks an equivalent in other languages. And, the multiple meanings of "belief" pose problems when it comes time for analysis and writing. For example, "acceptance of a proposition as true" is not the same as "trusting commitment." For Needham, the task of capturing and representing peoples' inner life was not feasible because beliefs do not directly mirror what people experience and cannot be directly relayed linguistically. In short, "belief" is more trouble than it's worth.

Part of Asad's (1993) critique was aimed at belief, echoing essays by Jean Pouillon, "Remarks on the Verb 'to Believe'" (1979), and Malcolm Ruel, "Christians as Believers" (1982). Again, Asad sees Geertz as exemplary of the problem. He argues that Geertz's use of belief is "a modern, privatized Christian" (47) concept because it invokes the Protestant theology that individual belief is necessary for salvation. The worry here is that the theological baggage from one religious tradition has infiltrated a concept being used for cross-cultural analysis.

Other critiques insist that belief misrepresents the actual compli-cated diversity of real religious lives. The term too narrowly signals fixed, pious commitment, which de-privileges other possibilities. What about the role of doubt and uncertainty in shaping religious commitment (Engelke 2007)? What about a more dynamic view that replaces a stable, fully internalized belief with an active, searching, but never fully resolved process of believing (Kirsch 2004)? What about the gaps between official religious proclamations (doctrines, creeds, vows) and the messy, lived commitments of everyday religious actors (Bielo 2011)? Mary Douglas, another prominent figure in the anthropology of religion, once wrote: "People do not necessarily listen to their preachers" (1966: 196).

Alongside these suspicions of belief we can raise a more straightforward, but no less powerful, critical question. On what analytical grounds can we rightly elevate belief as more central to religion than ritual practice, materiality (objects, built spaces, landscapes), forms of embodiment, or the authorizing processes that endow power and authority? (You might keep this question with you throughout the remaining chapters. Do you have a response now? If so, record it in your notes and revisit it following Chapter 6.) For now, I hope you see the substantial benefit to be gained from scrutinizing an individual concept, like belief, and an organizing category, like religion.

Box 1.2 Religion beyond religions

How might religion be present beyond the boundaries of defined religious traditions? A critique well established in both religious studies and anthropology is that the study of religion should not be confined to what we readily label as "religious." That is: does the world we label "non-religious" retain and foster religious practices, aesthetics, aspirations, and ways of world-making?

Jonathan Z. Smith, a historian of religion, wrote an essay titled, "Religion, Religions, Religious" (1998). In it, he performs a critique of "religion" similar to Asad, historicizing the category to reveal its social and intellectual baggage. However, his purpose was different. Asad wanted to demonstrate the limitations of "religion" for anthropologists. Smith wanted to demonstrate how, despite its history, this term establishes "a disciplinary horizon that a concept such as 'language' plays in linguistics" (281). Part of Smith's agenda is to suggest an open-ended horizon, one not tethered to what we label as "world religions" or "minor religions" (such a distinction, he points out, is a product of global power inequities). To see religion outside religions we must ask where else we find the elements and processes that are central to making and doing religion: separating what is sacred from what is profane, creating ritual structures, defining taboos, seeking purification, and so forth.

An example from the field of American religious history is Kathryn Lofton's *Oprah: The Gospel of an Icon* (2010). Lofton uses media content from Oprah Winfrey's empire to analyze how the religious aspects of popular, consumer, and celebrity culture transformed Oprah the person into Oprah the product. Her argument is not that Oprah somehow created a new religion, but that Oprah "plays religious" (9) through a variety of styles and strategies: from global missionizing to preaching to ritual transformation. (Ever think of a makeover as a kind of conversion?)

On your own, or with class colleagues, do some Lofton-inspired analysis of Oprah's online magazine: *O, The Oprah Magazine*.

- What religious themes are visible? How did you identify them as "religious"?
- How does *O* infuse religious themes into "non-religious" subjects?
- How would you design an ethnography of cultural production in Oprah's empire?
- How would you design an ethnography of cultural consumption in Oprah's empire?
- How would this ethnography help understand the way Oprah "plays religious"?

RELIGION–SECULAR, TANGLED DIVISIONS

As "religion" took its modern form in the 17th century, it was largely defined and understood vis-à-vis another category, "the secular." This was particularly true in civic contexts of government, education, and law. Peter van der Veer's work signals an important development within the anthropology of religion: studying the mutually effective intersections of religious and secular formations. With this development, the problem of defining religion achieves a particular distinction. It was the focus of early anthropologists like Tylor and Frazer who studied religious origins, and is now the focus of scholars who study how religion–secular entanglements operate on the world stage.

So, what is "the secular"? Our discussion thus far should suggest that an answer like "the non-religious" will not satisfy. Moreover, the secular has its own complicated past tied up in political claims of secularism, ideological claims of secularity, and scholarly claims of secularization. The sociologist Jose Casanova helps us grasp the secular with his book *Public Religions in the Modern World* (1994).

Casanova outlines three versions of secularization, only one of which is supported empirically. The first version is sometimes called the disenchantment thesis, which argues that modernity is a time of increasing rationalization (think: scientific progress) and, in turn, decreasing religious commitment (i.e., disenchantment). Empirically, this thesis seems to be quite wrong: the modern era has experienced drastic global increases in both religious commitment and religious diversity. Disenchantment also rests on the naïve idea that religion and science are locked in a zero-sum game for the loyalty of publics.

The second version can be called the privatization thesis, which argues that modernity will witness an increasing erosion of religion from the civic life of societies and be confined to the private life of individuals. This is the version Casanova rails most pointedly against due to the intense presence of numerous religious movements in modern public life. Among others, he names evangelical Christianity's influence on U.S. Congressional and Presidential elections, the transnational humanitarian work of faith-based organizations, Iran's 1979 Islamic Revolution, and the political success of Hindu nationalism in India.

Casanova's third version of secularization can be termed the differentiation thesis. The argument here is not about religious decline or private quarantine; it is that modernity successfully and permanently tattooed religion as something distinct from other social domains (e.g., politics, law, medicine, science). Moreover, secular differentiation marked religion as less legitimate than these alternatives for their respective tasks (e.g., governing, legal expertise, healing, and knowledge of the natural world). Religion lost the status of being a taken-for-granted worldview; it must now compete with other authorities for public trust and loyalty. We live in a secular age to the extent that the differentiation thesis is true.

Not surprising given his critiques we reviewed above, Talal Asad figures prominently in the anthropology of secularism. In his 2003 book, *Formations of the Secular: Christianity, Islam, Modernity*, he argues that the secular should not be conceived as merely the opposite of religion, nor as a kind of absence or invisible force. Secularism, just like religion, is a product of social action that is actively maintained, negotiated, and contested. A live question for anthropologists of religion is this: what varieties of secularism have been produced and what are their effects?

SECULARISMS

One place to begin a comparative anthropology of secularism is with the conditions produced within particular national contexts. van der Veer's *The Modern Spirit of Asia* (2014) is a good example; he contrasts the different forms of secular state development in China and India. Contrary to popular opinion, the 1949 Communist victory in China did not initiate a total anti-religious secularism. There was a long anti-clerical history pre-1949, in which traditions like Buddhism and Taoism were acceptable as moralities and philosophies but not as religions. The anti-clerical sentiment was far more opposed to official religious infrastructure (buildings, clergy, and other institutional forms) than it was Buddhist and Taoist ideas. The post-1949 state maintained this approach and added an ideology that "rationalism" and "scientism" were incompatible with "mysticism" and "superstition." Indian secularism, on the other hand, insisted on a policy of state non-interference in religion. The secular state was considered a solution to pluralist conflict (namely, between Hindus and Muslims) not a means of eradicating all institutional religions. India also promoted scientism, but unlike China's strategy of elevating science over indigenous traditions, India highlighted the scientific nature of indigenous traditions.

A second revealing comparison of divergent state secularisms is that of France and Turkey (Gole 2010; Stepan 2011). After the War of Independence in 1923, Turkey modeled itself after the 1905 French *laïcité* law, which strictly separates "Church" and "State" and bans religious expression in public life. (This differs from U.S. constitutional law, which is not grounded in a non-religious public sphere, but in state non-interference in the free exercise of religion and the prohibition of establishing a state religion.)

In France, majority and minority religions are (at least officially) given equal legal status. In Turkey, there are at least six crucial differences: a state office (the Presidency of Religious Affairs) exercises close control over the majority Sunni Muslim population (e.g., the state office writes the weekly sermon texts delivered in local mosques); for mosques that conduct public ceremonies, their clerics must be authorized and approved by the state; the state provides no financial support to minority religions and minority religions are not allowed to hold public ceremonies; graduates of public Islamic schools are not allowed to attend state universities, unless they are enrolled as theology students; teaching Islamic scripture to anyone under the age of 12 is prohibited; and, the state prohibits non-Muslim minorities from legally forming as religious organizations and from building sites of worship (Stepan 2011). While both France and Turkey claim the ideology of *laïcité*, they experience very different secular environments.

The comparisons of China–India and France–Turkey reveal that state secularisms can take widely different forms. Some very compelling ethnographic questions open up from this. How do legal and political realities create conditions in which religious, non-religious, and anti-religious actors exist in everyday life? How do these actors respond to problems of religious pluralism and multi-culturalism? How do religious actors engage the public sphere and what tensions must they navigate when doing so?

POST-SOVIET SECULARISMS

An exciting area of research has emerged around religion–secular entanglements in the post-Soviet states. From 1922 to 1991, the USSR existed as a socialist state that promoted scientific atheism and a negative bias against religion (see Luehrmann (2011) for a close analysis of how Soviet secularism was produced and consumed). In December 1991 the USSR dissolved, creating 15 new independent nations: Armenia, Azerbaijan, Belarus, Estonia, Georgia,

Kazakhstan, Kyrgyzstan, Latvia, Lithuania, Moldova, Russia, Tajikistan, Turkmenistan, Ukraine, and Uzbekistan. The post-Soviet bloc is an amazing case study in rapid social, political, and economic transformation. It also prompts fascinating questions about the relationship between the region's anti-religious Soviet past and the religion–secular entanglements of its possible futures. Consider three ethnographic examples of religious identity in different post-Soviet contexts. Taken together, what lessons do they suggest about the nature of religion amid post-Soviet secularisms?

Sascha Goluboff's ethnography, *Jewish Russians: Upheavals in a Moscow Synagogue* (2003), examines the lives of Orthodox Jews in post-Soviet Russia. Goluboff's fieldwork concentrated on a prominent Moscow synagogue whose demographics mirror Russia's post-Soviet social transformations. A local, primarily older, population of Russian Jews worships alongside visiting Western Jews (mainly from Israel and the United States) and Jewish migrants from former Soviet republics (mainly Georgia, Azerbaijan, and Bukharan from central Asia). During her fieldwork, approximately one fifth of Moscow's Jews were migrants. This owed to a more fluid national border and a more open religious environment following dissolution of the USSR. The ethnic and religious diversity at the synagogue made it a contested space, where competing claims to authentic Jewishness and citizenship clashed. In a compelling fieldwork moment, Goluboff captures a fistfight between an Israeli Jew, in Russia doing charity work and running a small business, and a Georgian Jew. Ostensibly, the fight erupted because the Georgian was not transitioning to a ritual space reserved for migrants as quickly as the Israeli wanted. In actuality, the fight was the boiling over of tensions between the synagogue factions. Neither side understood the fight in religious or ritual terms. Rather, it was interpreted through the lens of ethnic difference and differential access to the congregation's social and material resources.

Catherine Wanner's ethnography, *Communities of the Converted: Ukrainians and Global Evangelism* (2007), explores the phenomenal post-1992 growth of evangelical and charismatic Christianity in Ukraine. Kyiv is now home to Europe's largest congregation, a charismatic megachurch led by a Nigerian migrant named Sunday Adelaja. How did this happen? Ukrainian statehood included an opening of its borders, which were formerly defined by Soviet barriers. One effect was an incoming flood of well-financed North American missionaries. Given Ukraine's particular history and legal structure, Orthodox Christianity was not favored by the state as it was in places like Belarus and Russia. The result was a more open religious marketplace after independence. Evangelical churches, backed by those North American missionaries, gained public prominence by performing a variety of social services that were vacated when the state transitioned from socialism to market-based global capitalism. In turn, Ukraine has become a regional hub for training pastors and missionaries who then go into other post-Soviet nations, Western Europe, and elsewhere in the world.

Some of Ukraine's new missionaries end up in Kyrgyzstan, which was the ethnographic venue for Julie McBrien and Mathijs Pelkmans (2008) to explore how state secularists interact with Muslim and Christian missions. The Soviet anti-religious campaign in Kyrgyzstan focused on official religious infrastructure (e.g., church buildings), leaving intact the rituals of private life (e.g., home-based life cycle rites). This created a majority population that identified as both "Muslim" and "secular," in which being Muslim was transformed from a religious identity into an ethno-national identity. This population of secular Muslims responded quite negatively to the post-Soviet mission influx. Islamic missionaries were seen as extremists, associated with terrorist violence and gender discrimination. Christian missionaries were called a national threat. A striking example of secularist outrage came in a 2002 editorial in the Kyrgyzstan daily newspaper. The editorial bent Marx's famous "opium of the people" to an unintended end: "In small quantities [religion] is medicine. In large quantities it is poison" (McBrien and Pelkmans: 98). Through public proclamations like this, secular Kyrgyz sought to maintain a sense of national unity and political stability grounded in religious moderation.

Box 1.3 From public religion to religious publicity

The central claim of Casanova's *Public Religions in the Modern World* is that modern religions experience "deprivatization" amid a general backdrop of religion–secular differentiation. Religions are "challenging the legitimacy and autonomy of the primary secular spheres, the state and the market economy" (1994: 5). Casanova demonstrates that particular religious traditions in particular places have indeed gone public. But, what could we learn from an ethnographic account of religion in the process of going public? What would such an ethnography teach us about how religious actors envision a public audience, strategize to reach that audience, and create for themselves a public presence?

This is precisely what we have with Matthew Engelke's *God's Agents: Biblical Publicity in Contemporary England* (2013). Engelke's ethnography is about an independent Christian charity headquartered in England, the British and Foreign Bible Society. In particular, he focuses on a small staff at the Society, the Bible Advocacy Team. The Team's mission is to increase the Bible's presence in English public life. Engelke documents the Team at work—from office board rooms to city streets—as they brainstorm, plan, and implement strategies for generating "biblical publicity." The Team's labors reveal a recurring dynamic. They are convinced that the public they hope to reach is "secular": at best biblically illiterate and, at worst, hostile to all things Bible. They see their work as having to navigate a minefield of anti-religious sentiment.

In one of their public campaigns, the Team created a display for the Christmas season in the English town of Swindon. The organizing theme of the display was "angels in Swindon," a collection of angel figures placed throughout Swindon's major shopping district. The angels theme struck a happy medium for the Team, decidedly spiritual but not aggressively Christian. They would be suspended above the crowd, still visible, and breezes could be seen and heard moving across the wings. Engelke describes this campaign as producing an "ambient faith," where the angels work in material and sensory ways to index a general spirituality, rather than overtly proclaim a singular message. In their work of biblical publicity, the Team constantly tries to remix the strict differentiation of religious and secular space.

Work together with a class colleague to find and analyze two examples of religious publicity, each from a different religious tradition. Divide the labor equally, one example apiece. First, decide together what kind of project to look for. Some possibilities include: merchandising, radio programs, television programming, film production, museums, or sites of religious entertainment. Once you have your examples, meet up and address the following:

- What kind of public presence does each project seek to achieve?
- What strategies do they use to achieve that presence?
- Can you identify what audiences are being targeted? How?
- Is the secular signified in any way? How so and how did you identify the secular?
- What social conditions is this kind of project working within? What impacts do such conditions have on this example of religious publicity?

CHAPTER SUMMARY

In this chapter, we have critically examined "religion" as the organizing category for the anthropology of religion. Our first task was definition. Through comparing nine definitions, we saw that the act of defining can establish a normative posture toward religion, elevate particular aspects of religion over others, and mirror a scholar's theoretical commitments.

We then considered some anthropological critiques of "religion." Some scholars are suspicious of the entire category, seeing it as bogged down by ethnocentric baggage. We also explored critiques of "belief," a foundational concept in the anthropological study of religion that has generated its own suspicions. This section closed with a provocation: that religion can also thrive outside of defined religious traditions. My hope in presenting these critical voices is to illustrate how the study of religion is enhanced when we refuse to take ideas for granted or accept them at face value.

Our third section placed "religion" in dialogue with the category of the secular. Religion–secular entanglements are incredibly important for understanding the dynamics of religion in modern life. We compared the secularisms of China, India, France, and Turkey, demonstrating how state secular projects can differ widely from one another. To gain a fuller sense for how particular secular conditions impact religious life, we zoomed in ethnographically on three post-Soviet contexts. We concluded this section by sketching a useful distinction between public religion and religious publicity.

Ultimately, this chapter helps us think about the wide-ranging contents and boundaries of religious life. I placed a bet at the outset, that by the end you would appreciate why a definitive, succinct answer for what religion is would be unhelpful and, even, misleading. Did I bet wisely? My hope is that you are now better equipped to think critically about what religion is, what agenda(s) you might bring to studying religion, and why the anthropology of religion is pivotal to our comparative and holistic understanding of the human condition.

SUGGESTIONS FOR FURTHER READING

Along with the works cited in this chapter, consider these books and essays as productive next places to go. To follow up on "Defining is Theorizing," Brian Morris' *Anthropological Studies of Religion: An Introductory Text* (Cambridge University Press, 1987) outlines six theoretical traditions that engage the category of "religion" differently. An insightful review of the state of the field is Simon Coleman's "Recent Developments in the Anthropology of Religion" (in *The New Blackwell Companion to the Sociology of Religion*, Blackwell, 2010). For "Critiques of 'Religion,'" I recommend two edited collections. A 2008 special issue of the journal *Social Analysis* (52(1)) brings together 11 essays that interrogate the category "belief." *Magic and Modernity: Interfaces of Revelation and Concealment* (Stanford University Press, 2003) examines the many ways in which magical thought, practice, and institutions still operate in modern contexts. To further explore "Religion–Secular, Tangled Divisions," there is an excellent review essay by Fenella Cannell, "The Anthropology of Secularism" (*Annual Review of Anthropology*, 2010). Of the many valuable ethnographies that explore religion–secular interactions, a good one to start with is John Bowen's *Why the French Don't Like Headscarves: Islam, the State, and Public Space* (Princeton University Press, 2008).

DOING RELIGIOUS ETHNOGRAPHY

Are there particular challenges of doing ethnographic fieldwork that focuses on religious lives and worlds? This is one way to phrase this chapter's central problem. To begin, consider a widely cited book about an Afro-Carib healer living in New York City.

Mama Lola (Brown 1991) is "an ethnographic spiritual biography" (xiv), of a Vodou priestess from Haiti living in Brooklyn. The book is a product of 12 years (1978–90) of fieldwork and writing. It has won two prestigious awards: one from the American Academy of Religion and one from the American Anthropological Association. *Mama Lola* has provoked debate and discussion since its release, in part because of the intimate friendship that was forged between its author, Karen McCarthy Brown, and its central persona, Alourdes ("Ah-lood") whose nickname is Mama Lola.

Vodou priests and priestesses mediate between "the living" (Brown 1991: 4) and the spirits. They construct ritual altars to honor and invite the spirits. They use their body to host the spirits, channeling the unique gifts and powers of individual spirits to advise and heal clients who come seeking help. Vodou priests and priestesses assist people "with health problems and with a full range of love, work, and family difficulties" (5). Through her ethnography and her close relationship with Alourdes, Karen McCarthy Brown decided that she could not "remain a detached observer" (9). Three years into her research

Brown accepted Alourdes' invitation to become initiated into her Vodou family, changing Brown's personal and professional life. She began assisting Mama Lola in healing rituals, rather than only observing and documenting them. And, she started using Vodou when needing healing for her own troubles. "If I persisted in studying Vodou objectively, the heart of the system, its ability to heal, would remain closed to me" (10). In a follow-up essay, Brown (2002) reflected:

> My academic colleagues have raised questions. Have I lost my objectivity? Has my friendship with Alourdes biased my account of her family history, her daily life, and her spirituality? Has my participation in Vodou colored the way in which I present the religion? The answer to all these questions is a qualified Yes, although that doesn't disturb me as much as some of my colleagues wish that it did.
>
> (129)

The example of Brown, Alourdes, and *Mama Lola* does indeed raise pressing questions. How do we manage the intense relationships we forge through fieldwork alongside our scholarly research goals? What does it mean to do participant observation, a hallmark of ethnography, in religious settings where the stakes of participation can be especially high? What, if anything, is compromised or gained when a researcher finds personal value in the religion they are in the field to learn about? What is the proper place, if any place at all, for notions like "objectivity" or "bias" in doing religious ethnography?

As students, in this class or in the near future, you will begin doing the anthropology of religion by conducting your own research. When you do, questions such as these will arise in your own efforts to enter a religious community, come to understand some aspects about it, and then try to present what you have learned. Our purpose in this chapter is to give you a sense of the range of questions and issues that professional anthropologists engage with when doing religious ethnography and, in turn, prepare you for the same.

ETHNOGRAPHY AND RELIGION

The first major section of this chapter delves into a question that Karen McCarthy Brown confronted head on: What is my understanding of, and relationship to, the religion I am researching?

Before we go there, and to make going there more productive, we should say a few words about ethnography as an anthropological method and a way of knowing.

For cultural anthropologists, and for many scholars in religious studies and the sociology of religion, ethnographic fieldwork is the primary way we know what we know and the primary basis for building the representations we build. As a methodology, ethnography is distinguished by some fundamentals. First, it is about being there, wherever there is. Be it a short walk, a short drive, a short ride, a short flight, or a long flight followed by a long ride and a long walk, the ethnographer goes to the people they want to know about. Second, ethnographic fieldwork is extended, or long-term. Those are both relative terms; for some that means a year, for others several installments of multiple months, for others it can amount to several decades. In any case, there is no such thing as hurry-up, in-and-out, drive-by ethnography. Lastly, ethnography uses multiple techniques to collect data. I would wager that all ethnographers use some technique that is widely practiced (e.g., interviewing) and some technique that is tailored specifically to the unique details of their own fieldwork setting. But, all ethnographers rely on a complementary set of fieldwork practices that allow them to understand what it is they are studying.

To riff on an old joke: if you gather ten ethnographers in a room you'll probably get 11 opinions about how fieldwork ought to be done. A little exaggeration, but a little truth too. Different ethnographers frame the same methodology in different ways. Three typical framings are science, art, and craft. While some identify with only one of these, others combine two or all three. Personally, I like to think of ethnography as equal parts science, art, and craft.

Those who see ethnography as a kind of science highlight the fact that ethnographic fieldwork is conceived and conducted systematically. We are concerned with standards of reliability and accuracy. And, we contribute to comparative areas of research in order to advance theory. To see ethnography as art recognizes the human—indeed, passionately human—ways in which fieldwork produces knowledge inter-subjectively. In many ways, ethnographic success and failure hangs in the balance of how well relationships with fellow humans are established and nurtured. In *Mama Lola*, McCarthy Brown describes her work as "a social art form" (1991: 2), tethered to vulnerability, trust, excitement, regret, curiosity, patience, and other qualities that define relational life. Approaching ethnography as a craft calls attention to a simple, but profound, fact: while we always get better at doing ethnography, we never perfect it. Like the luthier or the winemaker, the only way for an ethnographer to improve is by constantly honing their craft. This has ramifications. For one, ethnography is time and labor intensive; it cannot be rushed and certain fruits come only through lengthy investment. Although it is laborious, a craft is also fundamentally creative. Crafts are living traditions; individual techniques become second nature, but the tradition itself is open-ended, prone to invention and adaptation.

To dwell on the methodological and existential dilemmas of doing ethnography, as we do in this chapter, reflects a sea change in anthropology. The critical turn, as it is often called, casts a reflexive eye on ethnography as a way of knowing. This turn emerged from several sources that coalesced in the 1970s and 1980s. Post-colonial, feminist, and critical race theories demonstrated how many methodological and theoretical frameworks across the social sciences reproduced dominant, often oppressive, ideologies (e.g., Said 1978). Dedicated anthropologists sought to reveal how fieldwork is rife with contingencies, ambiguities, uncertainties, and awkward relationships that are integral to the knowledge we produce (e.g., Rabinow 1977). Others reframed ethnography from being a research process where the anthropologist discovers cultural truths (like buried treasure waiting to be unearthed), to being an inter-subjective process in which our knowledge emerges from particular fieldwork encounters and dialogues (e.g., Dwyer 1982). And, a powerful critique emerged around the limitations and conventions of anthropological representations, primarily written texts (e.g., Clifford and Marcus 1986).

Anthropological critiques of anthropology and ethnography are about improving the discipline, not dismantling it. Iron sharpens iron (to pilfer a biblical phrase). The critical turn provokes anthropologists to be as self-aware as possible of the decisions we make at every juncture: what to research, why that topic/place/group was chosen, how to be in the field, and how to turn the hard won labors of fieldwork into words on a page (or, for ethnographic filmmakers, images on a screen). Whether an anthropologist sees themselves as an exacting scientist or a poetic humanist (or some creative integration of both), these issues are unavoidable and the quality of our science/art/craft is dramatically improved when we give them due attention.

The critical turn has been felt across the social sciences and in every area of anthropological inquiry, but "the nature of religion makes these questions especially biting" (Spickard and Landres 2002: 6). No ethnographic subject is uncomplicated, but anthropologists of religion can claim a unique set of challenges that are integral for producing successful work. Writing in the thick of the critical turn, anthropologist Paul Stoller said it this way: "the adequacy of applying social theory to anthropological data meets its greatest test [in] studies of shamanism, magic, and sorcery" (1984: 93). Simon Coleman, an English anthropologist who has published prolifically on pilgrimage and global Christianity, wrote: "Religion is a particularly difficult subject for the fieldworker to tackle, partly because of its nonempirical nature, and partly because of the rationalist assumptions of much social scientific scholarship" (2002b: 77). And Hillary Crane, in her writing about doing ethnography in missionizing settings, concludes: "Fieldwork conducted among missionaries is laden with unique difficulties and ethical ambiguities that highlight and exaggerate issues that arise in a variety of fieldwork contexts" (2013: 13).

There is something to this exceptionality. Anthropologists of religion are drawn into matters of life and death, moral standards and stigma, salvation and its alternatives, emotional ecstasy and vulnerability, spiritual wanting and fulfillment, healing and suffering, sacrifice and intensive dedication. All that is irreducible about religion as a human phenomenon fuses with our daily ethnographic labor. Moreover, some religious knowledge is understood in local contexts to be quite dangerous knowledge to learn and possess. It is not to be asked about or listened to lightly. Religious ethnography pushes the limits of the anthropological imperative of total fieldwork immersion. Ultimately, religious ethnography provides a sharp reminder that fieldwork is not simply a research task and a social endeavor, it is a moral, existential, and ontological project.

FOUR POSTURES

An enduring question in the anthropology of religion is what Matthew Engelke (2002) calls "the problem of belief." What do we, as ethnographers, allow ourselves to believe about the religious worlds we study? And, how do we square belief, non-belief, or ambiguity of belief with our anthropological goals of explanation, interpretation, and understanding? As we see below, while this does involve our personal commitments, it more crucially involves how we engage the truth claims we encounter. The problem of belief cuts to the bone of a central ethnographic tension: we are called to cultural immersion, yet going native is widely considered taboo and staying native even more so (Ewing 1994).

In response to this enduring question, we can distinguish four postures that ethnographers of religion can occupy. As you consider each, remember a few things. Each posture can be carried out in the field through a range of strategies. Second, none of these four postures offer any guarantee of success. Every one of them can be practiced very well and very poorly. Third, these postures can include or exclude several ways of obtaining information about the world: intellectual, bodily, emotional, and spiritual. Remember, too, that this chapter is geared toward doing anthropology: as you read ask what methodological consequences are likely to ensue from each posture. And, if you are actively doing research, ask what posture you find yourself in.

METHODOLOGICAL ATHEISM

Our first posture deals with the truth claims of religion only in social terms. "Methodological atheism" is an approach coined by the sociologist Peter Berger in his book *The Sacred Canopy* (1967). Berger explains it this way:

> It is impossible within the frame of reference of scientific theorizing to make any affirmations, positive or negative, about the ultimate ontological status of [religion]. Within this frame of reference, the religious projections can be dealt with only as such, as products of human activity and human consciousness, and rigorous brackets have to be placed around the question as to whether these projections may not also be something else than that.
>
> (100)

This posture insists on bracketing off religious truth claims on the grounds that social science research does not recognize non-empirical explanations. Anything you cannot directly observe or measure cannot be used to explain questions about religion. In practice, this means that the anthropologist approaches religion solely as a human product. Local religious explanations should not be accepted at face value, but instead should be subject to explanations rooted in empirical understandings of what is real, namely: social, economic, political, and material conditions (cf. Bialecki 2014).

Methodological atheism works according to a strict social constructionist logic: our sense of reality is achieved from living intersubjectively (i.e., a social world that is shared because we interact with other people). We form agreements about what is real and then act according to those agreements (Berger and Luckmann 1966). In the study of religion, this means that religious ideas and practices must be traced to a human origin, the social locations where agreements are made. Recalling Chapter 1, we can do this tracing work from a variety of theoretical orientations (for example, Marxist sociology or a Geertzian interpretive anthropology or an Asad-inspired genealogy of power relations). Whatever theoretical path we use to trace, the methodological atheist posture demands that tracing is the nature of our task and that our endpoint must be definitively social. In ontological terms, only humans and their products can be attributed a status of real-ness. Otherwise, we cease doing social science and start doing something else (theology, for example).

Methodological atheism need not be equivalent to personal atheism. A committed Buddhist and a skeptical atheist can both perform this posture because it is about leaving aside ("bracketing off") questions of truth altogether. Resolving the problem of belief means policing what is acceptable as an anthropologically valid explanation for religion as a human product. Berger, himself, was a committed Christian, but was firm in *The Sacred Canopy* that extra-sociological realities had no place in what he saw as a strictly empirical science (Yong 2012).

Ethnographers have used a methodologically atheist posture to a certain advantage while in the field. In a short, insightful article David Gordon (1987) discusses his research on groups affiliated with the Jesus People movement. Like many other evangelical Christian movements, Jesus People members place a heavy emphasis on missionizing and making new converts. Gordon was not a Christian and did not convert to Christianity through his research. However, he did not hide his non-Christian identity and, at times, would even use it by engaging his consultants in "empathic disagreement" (248). Like Berger, Gordon saw theological explanations as irrelevant for answering his research questions. Rather than obscure his personal commitments or stay silent about them, he used them to create productive fieldwork moments. He describes several instances where he actively argued with consultants as "good spirited affairs which we all enjoyed" (276). His goal was to elicit as much cultural knowledge and performance as he could. One strategy for doing this is to engage adherents in friendly debate about religious questions.

METHODOLOGICAL AGNOSTICISM

Our second posture also brackets off religious truth claims, but for a different reason. Ninian Smart (1973), a religious studies scholar, coined "methodological agnosticism" as an explicit alternative to Berger. These postures are similar in that they do not require researchers to take a stance on questions of religious truth. But, they absolve the researcher in different ways. Methodological atheism sees religious explanations as off limits, whereas methodological agnosticism declares questions of religious truth unknowable. The key difference is that methodological agnosticism approaches ontological questions about what is real as an ethnographic opportunity, not a taboo line to never cross.

Smart helpfully placed methodological agnosticism in dialogue with Berger, but this posture was already being used by anthropologists of religion (Bowie 2000). In *Theories of Primitive Religion* (1965) E.E. Evans-Pritchard (E-P) published a stinging critique of psychological and sociological theories (think: Freud and Marx) that approached religion solely as epiphenomenal (i.e., as only ever reflecting other, more fundamental sociological realities). E-P writes:

> There is no possibility of [the anthropologist] *knowing* whether the spiritual beings of primitive religions or of any others have any existence or not, and since that is the case he cannot take the question into consideration. The beliefs are for him sociological facts, not theological facts, and his sole concern is with their relation to each other and to other social facts. His problems are scientific not metaphysical or ontological. The method he employs is that now often called the

phenomenological one—a comparative study of beliefs and rites, such as god, sacrament and sacrifice, to determine their meaning and social significance.

(17; emphasis in original)

While this does resonate somewhat with methodological atheism, E-P differs on a crucial point. He maintains the focus on sociological facts, but he gives phenomenology ("meaning and social significance") primary importance, not explanatory social conditions. (You might also recall here the difference we discussed in Chapter 1 between Weber and Marx and Freud.) Unlike Berger, E-P does not call for "rigorous brackets," he simply declares religious truth claims to be unknowable. Consider an ethnographic example of methodological agnosticism in practice.

In *The Book of Jerry Falwell: Fundamentalist Language and Politics* (2000), Susan Harding uses ethnography and history to show how evangelical Christians in the United States compete with secular authorities for power, influence, and public loyalty. Harding openly discusses how her own status as a secular person shaped her fieldwork. For example, she recounts a car near-accident she experienced after leaving an emotionally intense interview:

Halfway across town, I stopped at a stop sign, then started into the intersection, and was very nearly smashed by a car that seemed to come upon me from nowhere very fast. I slammed on the brakes, sat stunned for a split second, and asked myself "What is God trying to tell?" It was my voice but not my language. I had been inhabited by the fundamental Baptist tongue I was investigating.

(33)

Her voice, not her language. As a non-Christian ethnographer working among conservative Christians, Harding was constantly the targeted audience of conversion efforts. In the interview preceding her almost accident, her interviewee had turned their conversation into an evangelizing session. Harding never converted, but she did use her experience to better understand the performance of conversion narratives ("witnessing") as a vital ritual in evangelical culture. "The first stage of fundamental Baptist conversion [is] to narrate one's life in Christian terms" (34). For her, focusing on how religious language gets internalized was a far more telling approach than "social scientists [who] scrutinize the external psychological and social conditions of converts" (35). By not denying or ignoring the way she had been "inhabited," Harding sought to challenge how "social scientists and professed unbelievers in general do not let themselves get close enough to 'belief' to understand it, or, for that matter, to see what it is" (36).

METHODOLOGICAL LUDISM

Our third posture engages religious truth claims not as a question to definitively answer, but as a role to play. For Andres Droogers, a Dutch anthropologist, methodological atheism and agnosticism are stuck, and therefore stick the scholar, at a standstill because they are caught between competing imperatives (1996). The rub is that methodological atheism's commitment to explaining religion as an expression of human social action cannot square with methodological agnosticism's desire to explain how religion works for adherents. Droogers calls this impasse "the deadlock between reductionists and religionists" (1999: 290). He coined his solution "methodological ludism," which he saw as a "both/and" solution, a way to incorporate both social conditions and the experiential real-ness of religion.

Methodological ludism is grounded in the work of Dutch historian Johan Huizinga (1955), who argued that the capacity for play (the ludic) is a pivotal aspect of the human experience. Play is serious business: vital for socialization, central to many social institutions, and the source of much joy and creativity. Droogers defines play as "the capacity to deal simultaneously and subjunctively with two or more ways of classifying reality" (1996: 53). The subjunctive is key, because it shifts the orientation from "as is" to "as if" (1999: 293), invoking the kind of deep immersion that characterizes virtual reality. Methodological ludism is about managing multiple realities: the scholar's personal biography, purely sociological explanations, the religious worlds encountered, competing voices within religious worlds, and secular critics. As fieldworkers, we can play by participating in each world *as if* it were absolutely real and true. The aim is to pretend in a fully committed way—to get caught up—but never lose sight of the fact that you are pretending. The ludist entertains a reality, but does not fully accept it.

For example, consider a co-authored article by Droogers and an ethnographer, Kim Knibbe, who put methodological ludism to work (Knibbe and Droogers 2011). Knibbe's fieldwork focused on a "Dutch spiritualist medium who claims to be a link between heaven and earth" (283). Physical healing was central to the medium's practice, as was "a quite positivist emphasis on proof. She encouraged people to be skeptical, to look for 'evidence' and record it" (284). As a scholar, Knibbe puzzled over how to deal with the truth claims being made by this healer and those who professed to having been healed. "Is the healing real? How does that matter for my analysis?"

Ultimately, they argue that methodological atheism unhelpfully "reduces beliefs to causes 'invisible' to the people involved, ignoring their agency and consciousness" and methodological agnosticism "meant ignoring what was right in the centre of what [the healer] was about ... the experience of 'the other side'" (290). For them, the ludic posture allowed and encouraged an experiential nearness to the phenomenon: Knibbe could play as if the healings were really real for the reasons the healer said they were. In this way, ludism responds to Harding's challenge of getting closer to belief, but on ontological, not merely cognitive, grounds. Still, at the end of the day methodological ludism requires no adjudication from the anthropologist on what really happened: if the "as if" was, in fact, the "as is."

METHODOLOGICAL THEISM

Our fourth posture is not content to play as if religious truth claims are real. Unlike the first three, the term "methodological theism" has no exact point of scholarly origin. The core of the approach is that the anthropologist can affirm the ontological reality of religious worlds through their research, not bracket off, ignore, abstain, or limit themselves to role play. This may strike you as provocative, if not controversial. It should! Methodological theism directly challenges some core social science tenets: to rely strictly on empirical data, to maintain a critical distance from what you are studying, to be skeptical of your own subjective experience.

One of the most vocal advocates for methodological theism has been Edith Turner. Turner was one half of a famed anthropological marriage. Her husband, Victor Turner, is a usual suspect in anthologies on the history of anthropology, namely for his studies of African ritual systems (see Chapter 4). The couple began doing fieldwork together in 1951 among the Ndembu of Zambia. In one book that resulted from this research, *The Drums of Affliction* (1968), Victor Turner analyzes the Ihamba ritual, a rite in which patients afflicted by contact with the dead are healed. He argued that the Ndembu use Ihamba as a social drama: a way to enact the political dynamics necessary for social cohesion.

Two years a widow and 31 years after the initial fieldwork, Edith Turner returned to the Ndembu in 1985 to research the Ihamba again (1992). She intended this to be a study in culture change: How was the ritual different three decades later? It all turned out quite different when she participated in the ritual, "instead of merely witnessing [and] saw with [her] own eyes a large afflicting substance, some six inches across, emerge from the body of the patient under the doctor's hands" (2). Her book *Experiencing Ritual* documents this experience and explains how affirming the affliction as real provides a fundamentally different approach to healing and religious ritual. Contra to her late husband's social drama argument, she was not content to view the ritual in functionalist terms. This led to a second ethnography, *The Hands Feel It* (1996), a study of Inupiat healers in northern Alaska. Here again, Edith Turner engages the healing practices as real in every way the healers say that they are.

Jean-Guy Goulet (1994) provides a second example, also set in Native North America, among the Dene of northwestern Alberta, Canada. He focused on Dene dreamers, "individuals who know an animal and who develop the ability to travel to and from the 'other land' through dreams and visions" (117). Goulet discovered that Dene epistemology required that the ethnography be done with an experience-near approach. "Dene informants are firm in their conviction that individuals, including ethnographers, who have not directly experienced the reality of dreams and visions do not and cannot understand Dene religion" (114). Because of this, Dene "exclude those who are not perceived as knowing from those among whom they discuss experiences of dreams, visions, and power" (ibid.). Something like traditional ethnographic interviewing, disengaged observation, and even uncommitted participant observation were unacceptable. Goulet's ethnographic success hinged on the fact that he too shared the Dene visions. Moreover, he saw his written ethnography as complete only when he put down on paper the details of the visions and dreams he experienced.

Turner and Goulet both practice a version of methodological theism, which critiques a strictly positivist scientific epistemology. They are most critical of an anthropology that treats religious experience as epiphenomenal: that is, by appealing to theories that only ever explain religion as reflecting psychological, sociological, symbolic, or materialist conditions. Methodological theism fosters a deep desire to not contort every field experience to fit the conceptual language of social theory, particularly those experiences that clash most dramatically with rationalist empiricism. Methodological theism is also quite dissatisfied with methodological ludism's flirtations with belief, but ultimate refusal to go all the way. As an ethnographic practice, methodological theism elevates the importance of experience, insisting that anthropological understanding must integrate intellectual, bodily, emotional, and multi-sensory ways of knowing. To borrow some words from Paul Stoller, whose ethnographic work in West Africa fits well alongside Turner and Goulet: "Just as painters, according to Cezanne and Klee, should allow the universe to penetrate them, anthropological writers should allow the events of the field—be they extraordinary or mundane—to penetrate them" (Stoller and Olkes 1987: 110). In this way, methodological theism seeks a permanent collapse of distance between researcher and researched, yet is firm that this collapse should not be dismissed by tropes like "going native."

CODA

In this section we outlined four postures that an anthropologist of religion might follow (Table 2.1).

In Box 2.1 you can work on applying these postures to an extended example. Before doing so, two observations will be helpful.

First, these postures shine a bright light on the tight coupling that exists between method and theory in ethnography. Each posture is better suited for some research questions than others. Methodological atheism leans in a stridently etic orientation: explaining religion as an epiphenomenal expression of outside conditions (e.g., economic markets, political hierarchies, social networks, ecological realities,

Table 2.1 Four methodological postures in the anthropology of religion

Posture	Ontological stance
Methodological atheism	*Bracketing*: religious truth claims are irrelevant for the job of the anthropologist, which is to approach religion as a human product and explain religion by appealing to social, cultural, or material conditions
Methodological agnosticism	*Bracketing*: religious truth claims are unknowable for the anthropologist, but this should not halt the search for religious meaning in the lives of adherents
Methodological ludism	*"As if" play*: religious truth claims should be engaged by the anthropologist as a site of play, a role to occupy in order to better understand religious experience
Methodological theism	*Experience near*: religious truth claims are fully knowable for the anthropologist, and should be sought as part of doing ethnography

psychological states). Quite the opposite, methodological theism is stridently emic: understanding religion in local terms, with local categories, and through local experiential registers. Methodological agnosticism and ludism attempt to chart a third way, one that integrates etic and emic forms of understanding and explanation. One could be dogmatic about this, and argue that anthropologists should identify with one posture and its appropriate questions. Or, one could see this as a question of the right tool for the right job. For example: What is the best way to study religious experience? Or: What is the best way to study schism within a religious institution? Or: What is the best way to study religious change over time?

Second, we can observe several points of contact and points of divergence among these four postures. One point in particular is a consistent way of distinguishing them: how they interact with the truth claims that emerge from religious worlds. This is a question of ontology. What is attributed the status of real-ness in the analysis? Is it limited to human productions (as methodological atheism would have it), or are non-human agencies recognized as well? After all, religious worlds are prone to celebrate God, gods, spirits, angels, demons, ghosts, the dead, ancestors, places, objects, spells, curses, and more. This is a question of both agency and evidence. If something is recognized as real in the methodology, what consequences does that have for the analytical attribution of agency, responsibility, and power? And, if we recognize something as real, what evidentiary basis do we use? Do we follow Edith Turner and listen to our sensual experience? In any case, it is useful to understand ontology as a clear dividing point among these four methodological postures (cf. Bialecki 2014).

Box 2.1 Being a (methodological) atheist, agnostic, ludist, and theist

On your own, or with course colleagues, try applying these four postures to an example. If you are doing research for a final project in your course, you can use data collected for that project. In addition, or instead of your own fieldwork, you can select a documentary film from the list below. Each film provides vivid examples of religion in practice:

- *Holy Ghost People* (1967; 53 min.): portrait of a rural, Appalachian Pentecostal congregation that practices snake-handling.
- *Shadows and Illuminations* (2010; 35 min.): portrait of the spirit world in Bali.
- *American Mystic* (2010; 80 min.): portrait of three healers—spiritualist medium, Wiccan priestess, and Lakota Sioux traditionalist.
- *Bad Friday: Rastafari after Coral Gardens* (2011; 63 min.): portrait of Jamaican Rastas and their collective memory of a violent clash in 1963.

After you have selected a film and viewed it, consider the following:

- For each posture, write one question about the religion being studied. How does each question reflect the assumptions and goals of the methodological posture?
- What kinds of data did you use to answer your questions? Are these data similar or different across the four postures? Did the questions require different kinds of knowing: did

you rely on different senses? observations? emotions? relationships?

- Ultimately, were you drawn to one posture over the others? Did you use them selectively or combine them? How comfortable were you working with each? Did any challenge your personal commitments? How so?
- Finally, return to the different aspects of the category "religion" we discussed in Chapter 1 (e.g., belief, ritual, embodiment, materiality, power, agency, etc.). How did these factor into your work with the four postures?

PRODUCTIVE REFLEXIVITY

In our opening discussion for this chapter, we highlighted the value of being reflexive when doing ethnographic fieldwork. The goal of this section is to think more thoroughly about the kinds of reflexive questions and practices that arise in the anthropology of religion. On a moment's pause, we can see that decision-making plays a prominent role in the day-to-day labor of doing religious ethnography: to confess or not, join the ritual or stand aside, believe or not, stay or go, sit or stand, close your eyes or keep them open, write the field note or wait, record or remember, pray or pass, sing or hum, weep or keep emotions snug to self. We will not tag every tree in this forest, but we will gain a good sense of the forest's scope and density. Three areas of interest organize our discussion: the *participant* portion of participant observation; the sometimes confusing, sometimes ambiguous, always important relationships we make and rely on during fieldwork; and, ethical dilemmas.

PARTICIPANT OBSERVATION

Our participation in the religious worlds we study can be limited: sometimes because we make the choice to abstain or temper the immersion, and sometimes because our access is curtailed or denied. Being reflexive about these decisions and events furthers our understanding of what we want to know about those religious worlds.

Katharine Wiegele (2013) studied charismatic Catholics in Manila, the Philippines. Like other charismatic Christians around the globe, the El Shaddai movement places a large emphasis on ecstatic worship, bodily experience, and healing. While attending one of the regularly held healing/counseling sessions, Wiegele confronted head on the charismatic ritual of being "slain by the Spirit." The ritual leader called Wiegele by name to the front of the room, laid hands on her, and slayed her:

> I fell into the arms of the group members, who laid me gently on the floor as they sang about the power of the Yahweh El Shaddai. It felt exactly as others have described—a growing, intense heat in the chest, a partial loss of consciousness wherein the ability to hear was retained, and shaking, clammy hands as I gradually returned to full consciousness.
>
> (89–90)

Wiegele did not convert after this experience, or at any point later in her work. She affirms the realness of the event in an experiential way, not in an ontological way as Edith Turner does. She did, though, use the event to reflect on the religious movement she was trying to understand: "my slaying gave me an appreciation of how complex such an experience is, how embedded its interpretation must be in personal history" (91).

Wiegele fully participated in charismatic rituals, bolstering her fieldwork in the process. This cannot always be the outcome. Tamir Erez (2013) studied Messianic Jews in Tel Aviv, Israel. Erez describes the congregation as religiously conservative, holding "a total and exclusivist definition of reality" (41). The congregation interpreted her ethnographic presence, defined by "empathic and nonjudgmental listening" (47), as evidence that she was seeking salvation. Initially, this eased the community's welcoming of her, but with time it became a problem. "The threat I posed by my empathic but nonbelieving position was more difficult for them to deal with than the regular stance of a critical nonbeliever" (49). On the one hand the community did not have a ready category to make sense of her continued presence but persistent non-conversion. Moreover, her continued presence went against the grain of their hope and expectation that enough time spent in the community would lead to conversion. After seven months, the pastor informed her that her research could no longer continue.

When the fieldworker is a religious outsider, like Wiegele and Erez, there can be a lot of fretting about how to do good ethnography while still being respectful and not giving a wrong or unethical impression. In her study of a Greek Orthodox pilgrimage site, Jill Dubisch (1995) wrestled with where to draw the line in her participation. She found it comfortable "to put money in the offering box and light a candle" (110) because it "allowed [her] to blend with the worshipers and neither stand out nor give offense" (111). However, kissing icons and making the sign of the cross was not comfortable, violating her personal sensibilities and signaling a false insider-ness.

These kinds of considerations are important: pragmatically, methodologically, and ethically. Sometimes, though, our fretting is for naught. In an essay about her fieldwork at a Taiwanese Buddhist school, Hillary Crane (2013) explains how her consultants did not share her worries. She hesitated about being a participant observer for the performance of a *chao shan* (a pilgrimage ritual involving strenuous mountain climbing). Her concern was that "as a non-believer, I would somehow diminish the event" (14). The nuns and fellow retreaters assured her that performing the ritual produces good karma, it doesn't matter what the individual intentions are.

The details of local religious life can also complicate our attempts to properly balance our dual roles as participant and observer. Matthew Engelke (2007) studied a charismatic Christian community in Zimbabwe with a distinctive history and theology. The Friday Masowe Church ("Friday" for their Sabbath day, "Masowe" for their founding prophet) call themselves "the Christians who don't read the Bible" (Engelke 2007: 2). Their rejection of the written biblical text is rooted in their general desire for an "immaterial faith" (3), that is a faith cleared of material objects and focused on an unmediated connection with the Holy Spirit. One result of this is that they rid worship spaces of as much materiality as possible (no Bibles, no books of any kind, no shoes, no buildings, only simple white robes). This included "any instruments for recording what went on: pens, notebooks, tape recorders, cameras, or videocameras. [He] was subject to the same conditions of experience as everyone else" (35). In Engelke's case, losing some traditional tools of the trade was necessary to gain closer access to, and a more robust understanding of, this religious culture.

RELATIONSHIPS

Whatever else ethnography is, it is about building, negotiating, losing, and celebrating relationships with fellow human beings. Very rarely do we study communities that are absolutely new and undefined, which means that the fieldworker will be placed into local roles and categories. These can range from the humorous to the dangerous, but in any case it is an integral part of our learning.

For those studying a missionizing religion, the outsider ethnographer almost always becomes a focus of conversion. This could be understood as an affront to ideals of neutrality and objectivity, but in fact it is an excellent opportunity. Susan Harding's work (discussed above) is a prime example. She used the event of her interview being turned into a witnessing session as the basis for understanding a genre of religious language and its central role in the religious culture. However, the target of conversion is not necessarily religious belief, as it was in Harding's case. In her work with North African Muslim migrants to Paris, France, Jennifer Selby (2013) explains how the focus was more on her body (e.g., fasting rituals, codes of dress, bodily comportment). Her acceptance into the community hinged more on abiding by these expectations than it did on professing a particular religious doctrine. This makes sense in an Islamic context where "a woman's appearance and social comportment acts as an externalization of her private, moral self" (46).

Being a religious insider is not the only role to consider. Erez (2013), again researching Messianic Jews in Israel, was not merely a religious outsider. Her broader social identity also mattered. Her presence was problematic, and eventually denied, because she reminded the congregation too much of "a typical young secular Israeli who has been exposed for the first time to [Messianic] beliefs but is not willing to embrace them" (41). In other cases, multiple social identities are the basis for confusion. Deana Weibel (2013) studied pilgrimage to a popular site in southern France (Rocamadour). Along with Catholic pilgrims, the religious history and natural beauty of the place draws sightseeing tourists and pagans who come for the "metaphysical, quasi-scientific energy" (Weibel 2013: 94). Her fieldwork relationships were not simply built around an insider/outsider status, but among these three common visitor roles as well as her own role as a non-Catholic, non-pagan, non-tourist ethnographer.

A local role that is not unique to ethnographers, but that has proven to be a revealing opportunity, is that of the apprentice. As a cultural newbie, the ethnographer is well placed to become a novice learner. Apprenticeship is time-consuming and strenuous, because you are expected to complete the same processes of initiation, development, and mastery as locals. Paul Stoller combined memoir and ethnography to write about his training as a sorcerer among the Songhay of rural Niger (Stoller and Olkes 1987). When the Songhay suspect sorcery or witchcraft attacks, they seek out a *sorko* (local healers and praise-singers to the Songhay pantheon). When he first started as an apprentice, Stoller's teacher assured him, "you must learn as we learn … we must teach you to hear" (Stoller and Olkes 1987: 29). Like all beginners he was considered quite ignorant about matters of the spirit world. To advance from being a novice *sorko*, Stoller "memorized magical incantations, ate the special foods of initiation, and participated indirectly in an attack of sorcery that resulted in the temporary facial paralysis of the sister of the intended victim" (ix). He goes on to report how he became the focus of a spiritual attack, which left him temporarily paralyzed in his legs. Stoller sorts through this intense experience using a methodologically theist posture, and he concludes that a root cause for being attacked was his involvement in a master–apprentice relationship.

ETHICS

Many examples we have discussed in this chapter are thoroughly ethical. Ethical issues and dilemmas are present in every stage of doing anthropology: designing research, being in the field, making sense of and producing a representation, and responding to your work's reception among multiple audiences (scholarly and not). Because religious worlds more often than not involve moral and ethical dimensions, scholarly ethics, personal ethics, and religious ethics come into contact.

How do we respond when confronted with religious ideologies that severely clash with our own worldview? This question can vex the veteran and novice fieldworker alike. Jessica Falcone (2012) had to ask this question in her work at a youth summer camp for fundamentalist Hindus living in Washington D.C. Hindu nationalism has grown among Indian migrants to the United States, perhaps because this religious–political movement fosters a nativist connection to the homeland and promotes ethnic solidarity among migrants living as ethnic minorities. At the summer camp, Falcone observed teenagers being taught an overt discourse of separatism that continually excluded Muslims and African-Americans. Doing this work meant finding strategies to tolerate "extremely uncomfortable" (184) interviews and conversations that centered on differences of religion and race.

The anthropology of religiously conservative women has proved challenging in this area. Saba Mahmood is a self-identified feminist who struggled to understand the women she met in Cairo who were involved in the Islamic piety movement (2005). From a Western secular liberal perspective these women clearly experienced gendered subordination and oppression on a daily basis. But, Mahmood was not content with a simple liberal/conservative explanation or to treat her ethnographic fieldwork as simply an extension of political discourse. Instead, she used the lives of these Muslim women to critically reflect on the nature of categories like freedom, authority, and agency that are so vital to secular liberalism. In her book *Mitzvah Girls* (2009) Ayala Fader wrestles with similar issues. Her research explored the socialization of "nonliberal" (1) ultra-orthodox Jewish women in Brooklyn, New York City. Like Mahmood, Fader wrote against the grain of secular liberal ideas about gender equity and individualism. Rather than use ethnography to critique Hasidic life, Fader sought to understand what distinguishes Hasidic femininity and why it makes sense to them.

Ethical struggles extend to the representational strategies we use. Marion Goldman (2002) did ethnographic research with women who had been part of the Rajneeshpuram community in central Oregon from 1981 to 1985. The Rajneeshee was a sectarian movement, a complex blend of spiritual philosophies and mystical traditions, led by the charismatic Bhagwan Shree Rajneesh. Devotees "chose to leave careers, friends, lovers, and sometimes families to follow a radical spiritual path" (Goldman 2002: 146). Rajneeshpuram became controversial soon after it began, becoming increasingly closed to the public and militarized. Goldman feared a negative blowback on the women if their identities were revealed. She decided to create composite character sketches rather than give the women pseudonyms, which is a common strategy to ensure anonymity. "I used the 11 women's own voices, words, and life experiences, mixing them to construct characters that protected the originals, without adding unnecessary fiction" (147). Goldman knew this strategy would lessen the legitimacy of her arguments among some scholarly audiences, but she decided it was the most ethical method. (See Chapter 5 for more on the Rajneeshee.)

Some anthropologists are religiously committed people, and it is an ethical decision to marshal that identity in your research. In a provocative essay, Brian Howell (2007) writes as a Christian anthropologist who studies Christianity. He argues that his Christian identity should be understood as a standpoint grounded in moral and ethical commitments, much like a feminist, Marxist, or secularist. Standpoint theory is itself a product of anthropology's critical turn, affirming that every view is a view from somewhere. Howell does not merely argue that his Christian identity is not an impediment to doing good anthropology. He goes further: "a Christian standpoint productively informs the practice of ethnography" (372).

As an illustration, he highlights his fieldwork with Filipino Baptists. He used his own background in American evangelicalism to understand how evangelical Christianity had taken on a distinctly local character in the Philippines. For example, their use of "belief" was not the same as what he was used to. They meant something much closer to a durable form of trusting commitment, not the individual affirmation of right church doctrine. As we discussed in Chapter 1, "belief" should not be taken for granted. Howell's example recalls Evans-Pritchard writing in 1965, who also saw personal religious faith as an anthropological aid (although, he was a Roman Catholic studying African witchcraft, not an evangelical Christian studying evangelical Christians). E-P quotes the Austrian linguist, anthropologist, and priest Father Wilhelm Schmidt (1868–1954):

> If religion is essentially of the inner life, it follows that it can truly be grasped only from within. But beyond a doubt, this can be better done by one in whose inward consciousness an experience of religion plays a part. There is but too much danger that the other will talk of religion as a blind man might of colors, or one totally devoid of ear, of a beautiful musical composition.
>
> (Evans-Pritchard 1965: 121)

CODA

Reflexivity, like theory, sharpens our ethnography. We improve by surveying the attentive work of others and, of course, through steady practice. What is at stake in all this? Being reflexive in religious ethnography enhances the richness of our data and the reliability of our analysis, in short: the trustworthiness of our science, the beauty of our art, and the quality of our craft.

Being reflexive is also about taking the transformative power of ethnography seriously. In her work with Pakistani Sufis, Katherine Ewing (1994) insists that we must allow our fieldwork to be capable of changing our vision of reality. I would add that understanding what changes we experience requires knowing what our starting points are. All the areas discussed here—participant observation, fieldwork relationships, and ethics—require some self-inventory. The first good reflexive move we can make is to ask who we are as we take ourselves into the field. This is why so many ethnographers, as part of their field notes or in a separate field diary, observe their personal changes (e.g., bodily responses, everyday perceptions, ethical stances). If you are working on a research project for your course, you might find a field diary to be an excellent way to track your own challenges to, and changes in, self.

Box 2.2 Religious ethnography and professional ethics

On your own, or with a course colleague, review the American Anthropological Association's (AAA) most recent "Statement on Ethics—Principles of Professional Responsibility." You should be able to find it at the following web address (though, if it moves to a new url you should be able to find it easily by searching online): www.aaanet.org/profdev/ethics/. The AAA code of ethics is written for all anthropologists, but how does it read using the particular eyes of a religious ethnographer? For each ethical principle (there were seven in the 2012 statement) consider these questions:

- Given what we outlined in this section, could religious ethnography pose special dilemmas for following the code?

- Do examples of religious ethnography exemplify the need for this code?
- Could different religious cultures—say, conservative and liberal expressions of the same religious tradition—require different applications of this same code?

CHAPTER SUMMARY

In this chapter, we have explored the particular challenges of doing the ethnography of religious worlds, lives, and communities. Ethnographic fieldwork is the central methodology for cultural anthropologists, and is also widely practiced in religious studies and the sociology of religion. Anthropology's critical turn has instilled the importance of doing ethnography with a reflexive eye turned on our own practices and decision-making. We do this for the sake of sharpening our science, art, and craft.

All religious ethnography must confront the "problem of belief" (Engelke 2002). There are four dominant postures that we might choose from or seek to integrate: methodological atheism, agnosticism, ludism, and theism. Each posture has distinct recommendations for how ethnography should be done and implications for engaging the day-to-day labor of fieldwork. Each posture also highlights the tight coupling of method and theory. Perhaps the most telling feature that divides them is their ontological stance—what their analysis recognizes as real and anthropologically relevant.

Fieldwork is hard work, but it is also revelatory work. This is keenly powerful for religious ethnography, as we confront matters of life and death, moral normativity and stigma, salvation and its alternatives, emotional ecstasy and vulnerability, spiritual wanting and fulfillment, healing and suffering, sacrifice and intensive dedication. Fieldwork revelations come, in part, through practicing reflexivity and we highlighted three areas of reflexive inquiry: the dilemmas of participant observation, the formative nature of fieldwork relationships, and the unavoidability of fieldwork ethics.

Ultimately, this chapter demonstrates the need to be conscientious religious ethnographers. Each of the remaining four chapters has an ethnographic imperative, and you will encounter a wide range of religious traditions, lives, worlds, and communities. As you read on, return to the issues and questions raised in this chapter. What methodological posture is at work? How is the method–theory relationship visible? What fieldwork decisions set the stage and allow for arguments and findings? What ethical dilemmas did the anthropologist confront?

SUGGESTIONS FOR FURTHER READING

Along with the works cited in this chapter, consider these books and essays as productive next places to go. To follow up on "Four Postures," one of the early ethnographic challenges to methodological atheism and agnosticism is Jeanne Favret-Saada's study of witchcraft in rural France, *Deadly Words: Witchcraft in the Bocage* (Cambridge University Press, 1980). Joel Robbins' "Anthropology and Theology: An Awkward Relationship?" (*Anthropological Quarterly* 79(2), 2006) is an insightful essay on how anthropologists can engage with the work of theologians. Jon Bialecki's "Does God Exist in Methodological Atheism?" explores the ontological implications of different methodological postures (*Anthropology of Consciousness* 25(1), 2014). To continue with "Productive Reflexivity," I recommend three edited volumes. *Personal Knowledge and Beyond: Reshaping the Ethnography of Religion* (New York University Press, 2002) gathers 19 essays by anthropologists, sociologists, and religious studies scholars reflecting on the methodological and epistemological aspects of doing the ethnography of religion. *Extraordinary Anthropology: Transformations in the Field* (University of Nebraska Press, 2007) features 17 anthropological essays on what happens when ethnographers have profound personal experiences during fieldwork. *Missionary Impositions: Conversion, Resistance, and Other Challenges to Objectivity in Religious Ethnography* (Lexington Books, 2012) collects eight essays examining the dynamics of fieldwork in missionizing contexts.

3

BODIES, WORDS, AND THINGS

Picture a religious scene in your mind's eye. What is there? What is happening? Are there people? What are they doing? Is it *only* people?

My guess is that the scene you conjured involves people actively doing something, and that it is not people alone. Religious practice is about performing many kinds of action: singing, dancing, clapping, laughing, shaking, being still and silent, reading, writing, speaking, eating, drinking, working, and traveling. Religion-in-practice also finds people surrounded by stuff: books, clothes, jewelry, buildings, and a countless variety of natural and human-fashioned objects.

Here's the trick: performances and stuff are not incidental. They matter greatly for the fundamental goals of religious life. This raises a central research problem in the anthropology of religion: how do individuals and communities use the visible, tangible, and visceral to engage the spiritual. In short, how is the immaterial materialized?

MEDIATION

"Bodies, words, and things" is this chapter's title, and those are the categories that organize our discussion. Before we start exploring ethnographic examples, some conceptual orientation will help.

What anthropological tools can we use to understand how the immaterial is made material? "Mediation" is an especially useful concept, which we can define as: the use of social resources to structure our experience, understanding, and communication.

An interest in mediation reflects the "media turn" in the anthropology of religion (Engelke 2010). In Chapter 1 we discussed how the category "religion" has historically been attached to distinctly Christian assumptions. For example, prioritizing interior states like belief reflects the Protestant theology of salvation through doctrinal confession. Interior states are certainly important for many religious traditions, but the study of religion should not be reduced to them. The media turn elevates our attention to the non-interior elements of religious life. Three key examples are bodies, words, and things. This also enables us to ask what kinds of relationships exist between belief and materiality. How are different media used to create, share, and reflect on interior states?

We can observe three qualities of mediation upfront. (1) Mediation is a process. It is not something an individual or a group attains once and for all. Religious mediations are made, remade, taught, adapted, negotiated, and contested. (2) Mediation is social. It is shared with others and publicly visible. Because of this, religious mediations can become the object of critique and praise. This works in tandem with mediation as process: critique and praise are ways of remaking and contesting. (3) Mediation is about performance. Art, dance, song, writing, and any other way of making the immaterial material are ways of saying something. Performances are ways of commenting about self, community, belonging, aspiration, and even religiosity itself.

All religious worlds rely on mediation. We see it at work when Eastern Orthodox Christians interact with theologically significant architecture and consecrate food. It is at work when pious Muslims listen to cassette sermons as they walk down the street. It is at work when Hasidic Jewish men wear *tallit* (prayer shawls) and read aloud from the Torah. It is at work when Vodou priests and priestesses fill altars with images and objects. It is at work when Appalachian Pentecostals handle rattlesnakes and pray by laying hands on radios and TVs. This chapter will explore a variety of ethnographic examples, all of which affirm the significance of making the immaterial material.

Box 3.1 Applying mediation

On your own, or with course colleagues, spend some time engaging this concept of mediation.

- Do you grasp the basic idea and purpose of the concept?
- Why might this be a necessary concept and what is forfeited by approaching religion without it?

The best way for concepts to come alive is through application. Use one of the documentary films from the list below to see mediation in action. How are adherents using mediation to make religious life work? How are the three qualities of process, social, and performance evident? If you are working with a course colleague, discuss your answers and observations together.

- *Finding God in the City of Angels* (2010; 116 min.): portrait of the impressive religious diversity in Los Angeles, California.
- *Embrace* (2011; 55 min.): portrait of Tibetan Buddhist monks, tantric yoga, and the natural landscape.
- *Hell House* (2001; 85 min.): portrait of a Pentecostal congregation in Texas, and their production of an annual alternative Halloween haunted house.

BODIES

We humans have always had one material resource at the ready: our bodies. Marcel Mauss, an influential French anthropologist (and a nephew of Emile Durkheim), called the body our "first and most natural instrument" (1935 [2006]: 83). Religious worlds are thoroughly embodied. Bodies are used to establish that the spirits are present, to make religious identities visible, and as a site of mastering devotional tradition. And, particular bodies are constantly remembered and imagined: a muscular Jesus for some charismatic Christians, a laughing Buddha endowed with a bulging pot belly. Consider three issues for thinking about the body as a form of religious mediation: learning, discipline, and the senses.

Learning. In Mauss' essay "Techniques of the Body" we learn that an integral aspect of socialization is the way bodies are trained. You have experienced this first-hand. Certain situations provoke instinctual, habitual, and seemingly automatic bodily responses. Just as we shiver when it's cold, we ensure an upright posture when confronted with authority. Feelings of awe bring goose pimples to our skin. Mauss' great insight is that bodily responses are culturally variable. To capture these instinctual, trained responses he used the term "habitus," which refers to our set of learned dispositions. A generation later, Pierre Bourdieu (1977) elaborated on the nature of habitus and how dispositions influence actions. Bourdieu argued that bodily learning occurs differently within, as well as across, cultures. There can be a specific habitus for social classes, ethnic groups, and genders. In turn, we should expect bodily learning to vary among religious communities and traditions.

Discipline. Bourdieu was also very interested in social relationships like dominance and subordination, and how power relations are reproduced through our learned dispositions. After all, you do not ensure that upright posture for everyone all the time! The French philosopher Michel Foucault also had an abiding interest in power relations. Instead of "learning," Foucault preferred the term "discipline" to understand how the individual body is the target of powerful institutions (e.g., schools, hospitals, prisons). In her ethnography *Politics of Piety* (2005), Saba Mahmood studied the Islamic revival in Cairo, Egypt. She used Foucault's notion of discipline to understand how Muslim women gain and teach piety. Mahmood challenged the common assumption that bodily habits are products of already established beliefs, arguing that Muslim women discipline their bodies through prayer, fasting, and other rituals as a way of cultivating beliefs.

Senses. Sight, sound, touch, smell, and taste are vital to religious life. Leigh Eric Schmidt, an American religious historian, explored the relationship of the body, senses, and religion in his book *Hearing Things* (2000). Schmidt focuses on the religious diversity of the United States in the 1700s and 1800s, including Methodists, Mormons, and Shakers. A key lesson of the book is that the senses are constantly being ranked, and re-ranked, in religious experience. "Devotion has always been deeply bound up with the refusal and deflection of the senses, whether plugging the ears, averting the eyes, or avoiding the touch, [we are] constantly negotiating the temptations of the body through the body" (viii). As anthropologists thinking cross-culturally, we should be cautious of Christian-inflected themes like "temptation." That said, recognizing sensorial hierarchies is a very helpful analytical move.

From here, we explore some ethnographic examples of how religious worlds use the body to mediate identities and spiritual ambitions. To do so, we profile three areas of comparative research: food, music, and blood. For each example below, ask how issues of learning, discipline, and the senses are at work.

FOOD

Everyone eats. And, anthropologists use food to unlock all manner of cultural puzzles, from what counts as food to the way dining practices reveal social structures and the symbolic power of food and eating. Relationships between food and the body work out in staggeringly different ways across cultural contexts, and religion poses no exception. Religious communities use food to say things about who they are, who they want to be, what's wrong with the world, and how the world can change. For some readers, food and religion will not be a surprising coupling. Jewish norms about keeping kosher, the preparation of food for deities in Hindu worship, or rituals of fasting all might come to mind. Consider two ethnographic examples, and how their contrast illustrates the entanglement of food, religion, and bodily mediation.

Carolyn Rouse and Janet Hoskins (2004) use food to understand the transformations in one religious community: African-American Sunni Muslim (AASM) women in Los Angeles, California. Rouse and Hoskins tell an intertwined story about competing Muslim identities, blackness as a racial identity, and social change. The authors focus on three periods of AASM history: 1930–75, the Nation of Islam's founding to the death of Elijah Muhammad, long-time leader of the movement; 1975–2001, which saw large increases in Sunni membership; and, post September 11 2001, when all American Muslims became subject to negative stereotypes about global Islamic terrorism. Each period had a different defining mood: a defiant racial separatism (1930–75); a desire to demonstrate the compatibility of being American, African-American, and

Muslim (1975–2001); and, a post-9/11 anxiety about overt religious display (e.g., female veiling).

For AASM women "perceptions of food act as a metaphor for an evolving gender, race, class, and citizenship identity politics" (Rouse and Hoskins 2004: 228). One changing food perception occurred around the status of "soul food," a cuisine developed among African-Americans during the slave period using meats (e.g., chicken livers) and vegetables (e.g., field greens) discarded by white slave owners. In the 1960s and 1970s soul foods were marketed to African-Americans as a kind of heritage cuisine. The Nation of Islam denounced soul food as part of racial suffering and suppression, making soul food taboo because it polluted black bodies and contributed to marginalization. In the post-1975 era, Sunni Muslims embraced soul food as a way to embrace a distinctly black American identity. "Southern cooking was re-appropriated as a tribute to African American agency during slavery and Jim Crow" (Rouse and Hoskins 2004: 244). In other words, soul food was transformed from a spiritual threat among the Nation of Islam to a proud cultural tradition among Sunni Muslims.

Our second example is also about soul food, blackness, and religion, but tells a very different story. In his ethnography *Thin Description* (2013), John Jackson writes about the African Hebrew Israelites of Jerusalem (AHIJ). The AHIJ is a transnational community who claim to be direct descendants of the ancient Israelites depicted in the Jewish scriptures. Like many other Jewish communities, they call modern day Israel–Palestine their ancestral homeland. An AHIJ community settled in the southern Israeli city of Dimona in 1969, and continue to thrive there today. Members living in the United States make pilgrimage to Dimona whenever possible. However, the Israeli state rejects their genealogical claims and for many years denied their state citizenship.

A core AHIJ belief is that humans, along with the earth, are designed by God to live forever. Immortality! They believe the covenant between humans and God was broken by Adam and Eve, which they seek to restore through bodily and spiritual purification. Where does food fit into this picture? For the AHIJ, purification begins with the human body and a "careful parsing of what and when to eat" (Jackson 2013: 216). This makes food "the cornerstone of their entire [cosmological] project" (217). In a literal reading of biblical text, they proclaim a divinely ordained veganism by quoting Genesis 1:29: "Then God said, 'I give you every seed-bearing plant on the face of the whole earth and every tree that has fruit with seed in it. They will be yours for food.'" Along with strictly eliminating animals and animal by-products from their diet, the AHIJ "'holistic health maintenance' program mandates recurring no-salt days, 'solar food' days (food cooked directly and exclusively by the sun's rays), Shabbat fasting, periodic enemas, and physical exercise at least three times a week" (Jackson 2013: 5).

Where does soul food come in? The AHIJ covenant seeks to restore the whole world, not only themselves. They want to teach and share their holistic health maintenance as widely as possible, beginning with their racial brethren. One strategy for fulfilling this covenant has been to start an international chain of vegan soul food restaurants. Through the modern mechanism of entrepreneurialism, AHIJ communities pursue personal and universal purification, one bowl of vegan "mac-n-cheese" at a time.

African-American Sunni Muslims and African Hebrew Israelites of Jerusalem: two religious communities who use soul food to make defining statements about who they are. Both groups emphasize the integration of race, religion, and food. They emphasize blackness, and create regulations around what the racialized body needs. Both groups also work with themes of purity and taboo, which are classic themes in the anthropology of religion. In her famous study of comparative religion *Purity and Danger* (1966), Mary Douglas demonstrated how religious traditions throughout the world and throughout history divide life into categories of clean and unclean. Douglas defines dirt as "matter out of place" (36). She argued that a central feature of religious life is to embrace what is clean and create rituals to make clean what is dirty. Note how this plays on the sense that "religion" is about establishing order. For African-American Sunni Muslims and African Hebrew Israelites of Jerusalem, you are what you eat and consuming unclean things endangers you. Here, we see how fundamental goals of religious life can be grounded in bodily mediation.

MUSIC

Food is about changing our bodies, but we can also consider how bodies move. Body moving happens in a variety of religious ways, from travel to trance to sex. For now, we'll focus on dance. Again, we use a contrast to illustrate how bodily mediation works. This time, the contrast comes from the same ethnographic study.

In *The Color of Sound* (2013), John Burdick compares three groups of Christian musicians in Brazil's largest city, Sao Paulo. Burdick's ethnography presents us with another cultural variation of blackness. In Brazil, male *negros* and female *negras* are the Afro-descendant population who are marked as racially different from Portuguese descendants (*branco*), mixed-race (*moreno*), and indigenous (*indigenas*) groups. *Negros* and *negras* are a structurally marginalized population in Brazil: working in low-wage jobs, living in unstable and often dangerous neighborhoods, and discriminated against by *brancos* and *morenos*. The majority of *negros* and *negras* are now *evangelicos*: a religious category in Brazil that encompasses several Protestant denominations and traditions. Burdick asks an important question about this racial–religious identity: "To what extent may *evangelicos* develop black pride from within the ideological matrix of evangelical Christianity" (2013: 11)? To answer this, he focuses on a certain kind of religious actor: musical artists. Sao Paulo's *evangelicos* perform in three musical genres: rap, samba, and gospel singing. Ultimately, artists from these three genres differ in how they construe racial and religious authenticity. A central part of their difference is how they understand and engage the body. Movement cannot be understood apart from local understandings of voice, performance, and authenticity.

In gospel rap, physicality responds to affective intensity and sincerity. If you are moved, then you move. But, what does a good rap voice sound like? How is quality judged? The rapping voice is about delivery, not sonic pleasure. Burdick describes the voice of one gospel rapper this way: "it is a hypnotic voice, one that commands attention, makes you want to listen; but it is far from a beautiful voice: it cracks and creaks and squeaks and becomes breathy" (2013: 82). In the place of technical precision, a masterful rapping voice is "about practicing articulatory skills, such as flow, speed, and enunciation— and, of course, honing the content of the message" (85). Good rap must say something meaningful. This is what makes listeners to gospel rap dance.

The gospel singing voice is nearly the opposite of *evangelico* rap. There is a "hyperconsciousness of the voice's physicality" (137). Gospel singers train by exercising and disciplining the material elements of their voice: sensations of the larynx, vibration, controlled breathing, projecting, positioning lips and tongues. Unlike rap, gospel singing is explicitly racialized. The qualities that are said to make for great singing are also said to be part of blackness. Authenticity returns, but in different form. Here, it is judged by racial identity not a sincere and content-driven performance. Listeners dance when the aesthetics of the black voice are powerful.

Samba is different yet again. Rap and gospel singing were both imported to Brazil from the United States. Samba is a domestic product, widely considered a symbol of Brazilian nationalism. So, what does good samba sound like? "The key quality one listens for in a sambista is the fit between melody and lyric and the minimal ability of the singer's voice to deliver the latter" (106). Minimal is the key word. Neither performative expertise nor vocal proficiency is required. A good samba voice gets out of the way, lets rhythm take over. In turn, dancing is far more central to samba than any understanding of voice. For this reason, despite its privileged position as a national symbol, *evangelicos* say samba is more dangerous than rap or gospel. Samba dancing is synonymous with party culture, nightlife, sensuality, and sexuality. When attending a church worship service where gospel samba was played, Burdick observes how dancing worshippers "carefully avoid gyrating" (110). The hips don't lie.

BLOOD

Food and dance illustrate how religious mediation works by how bodies are changed and how they move. For a final illustration, let's push our thinking about bodies even further. Blood does this. Part of mediation's analytical payoff is that it highlights interior–exterior relations. We could be very literal here. Blood is a material substance that exists inside us. It can be made exterior for religious purposes; perhaps by blood donation as a charitable act. But, culturally speaking, blood cannot be reduced to its material status. Blood signifies. Blood is the source of confusion and disagreement. Consider two ethnographic examples, and what their contrast has to say about blood as a form of religious mediation.

The African Hebrew Israelites of Jerusalem are not the only Jewish community to be excluded by the Israeli state. In *One People, One Blood* (2009) Don Seeman explores the example of

Ethiopian-Israelis (or, as they call themselves, Beta Israel). In the 1860s, British colonialists in Ethiopia reported discovering a large group of Black Jews who claimed to be descendants of the Lost Tribes of ancient Israel. Like most other African populations who encountered British colonialism, they were missionized and many converted to Christianity. Some did not convert, and generations later the descendants of many who did convert renounced Christianity and reclaimed a Jewish identity.

In the 1980s, at a time when Ethiopia experienced widespread poverty and political instability, Beta Israel called for a return to their ancestral homeland, modern day Israel–Palestine. In two "Operations" conducted by international military and humanitarian coalitions— Operation Moses in 1984 and Operation Solomon in 1991—Beta Israel were flown into Israel as refugees. Despite a 1977 ruling by the Israeli state that the Law of Return did apply to Beta Israel (unlike the AHIJ), many Israeli Jews discriminated against Beta Israel as not authentically Jewish.

On what basis do Beta Israel claim Jewish authenticity, and Israelis dispute their Jewishness? It is not about affirming certain doctrines or practicing certain rituals. It is about blood, descent, kinship. Beta Israel claim a genealogy of being descended from the Israelites depicted in the Jewish scriptures; their deniers reject that claim. Some Israeli Jews say they are just "self-interested 'economic refugees'" (Seeman 2009: 14). Others say their Judaism is suspect because their recent ancestors converted to Christianity. Legally, Beta Israel can be citizens of the state. Citizenship is mediated by governmental bureaucracy. Religious identity is mediated by blood, and blood is not so easily discerned. This came to a bloody climax in 1996 when an Israeli newspaper "revealed publicly for the first time that the Israeli blood bank administered by *Magen David Adom* (Red Star of David— Israel's equivalent of the Red Cross) had been routinely destroying blood donations made by Ethiopian-Israelis" (150). Protests amassed in Jerusalem, some turning violent. The "Blood Affair" was a vivid reminder of Beta Israel's marginal status, the symbolic and material power of blood, the ambiguity of authenticity, and the entrenched nature of racial ideologies.

The Church of Latter-day Saints (Mormons) presents a different example of contested religious identity, kinship, and the significance of blood. Fenella Cannell (2013) conducted fieldwork with

Mormons in the United States. Cannell explores how Mormons maintain several relationships with blood and descent.

To begin, Mormon scripture places the Latter-day Saints (LDS) of America in the genealogy of the Lost Tribes of Israel: "The LDS prophet Lehi is said to have travelled to the New World, and to be descended from Ephraim, son of biblical Joseph" (2013: 85). Second, it is a religious obligation for every Mormon to compile an extended family genealogy. Members "take the names of these ancestors to the Mormon Temple [in Utah] where salvation and blessings can be offered to them through ritual means" (83). Third, there is a kind of "religious–social elite" (83) among Mormons whose family lineage reveals direct descent from either Joseph Smith (the founding prophet from the 1820s) or Brigham Young (the prophet who led the Mormon settlement of the American West in the 1840s).

At least until the late 1970s, compiling family genealogies was a source of racial anxiety. LDS hospitals were among the very first in the United States to set up organized blood banks, and "from 1943 to 1978 'black' and 'white' blood stores were kept, because of the fear among white Mormons that even one drop of 'black blood' might render one ineligible for the priesthood" (86). Finally, pre-occupations with lineage and kinship resurface in contexts of child adoption: "LDS sometimes think of kin, including adopted kin, as having 'chosen' each other ... a notion which limits the idea that kinship is simply physically determined, or that adoption is 'less' than biological kinship" (89). Blood mediates in several ways for Mormons: to narrate religious history, perform religious duty, assign social status, and define kinship.

Box 3.2 Religious bodies

On your own, or with class colleagues, reflect on the relationship between religion, bodies, and mediation. Here are a few questions and exercises to help.

- Begin with the issues of habitus, discipline, and the senses. How did you see these at work in the examples above? How do they help you understand the role of the body in religious mediation?

- Recall the example of vegan soul food. Search online for an African Hebrew Israelite vegan soul food restaurant. Once you find one, look at the menu. How does the menu perform AHIJ identity? How does it reproduce ideas about purity and danger?
- Recall the example of Brazilian gospel rappers, singers, and sambistas. Search YouTube for videos of performances in each genre. View an example of each and discuss how themes of body, voice, dance, and mediation are evident.
- Recall the examples of Beta Israel and Mormons. Note that both include a case of blood banks managed according to racial logics. What are the similarities and differences between these two cases, particularly with regard to questions of authenticity?
- Are you conducting a research or fieldwork project for your course? If so, how does bodily mediation work in your project? ✓

Bodily mediation also helps us think about broader themes in the anthropology of religion. For example:

- Note how our discussion of bodily mediation continually returned to racial identity. Why might this be? How do ideas about race inform the role of bodies in religion, and vice versa?
- Note how our examples of bodily mediation blur binaries, such as a strict divide between sacred and profane (e.g., an international chain of vegan soul food restaurants; gospel samba). Why might the body be especially good for blurring binaries?
- Note how bodily mediation is one strategy religious communities use to construct and assign authenticity. Why might the body be especially good for engaging debates about authenticity?

WORDS

Prayer, preaching, prophecy, chanting, casting spells, exorcizing demons, divination, accepting oaths and vows, confessing, witnessing, inviting spirits, singing: what do these practices have in common? They are all fundamentally linguistic religious performances. In some traditions, literacy practices are also important (e.g., evangelical Protestants doing group Bible study, orthodox Jews reading the Torah aloud). Religious language is an excellent way to understand both religion and language because it "can involve people's most extreme and self-conscious manipulations of language, in response to their most powerful intuitions about agency" (Keane 2004: 431). In this section, we explore the dynamics of religious mediation by asking how religious language helps remember, transmit, and reflect on beliefs, values, and senses of self, community, and the cosmos. This analysis begins with two key ideas about the nature of language: pragmatics and verbal art.

First, this section highlights the pragmatic function of language. You can think about this as contrasting with the referential function, which is about how we use language to describe a reality. But, language is not merely a descriptive tool. Language can also help create a reality. This is what the pragmatic function is about, the way we use language to make things happen. J.L. Austin, a philosopher of language, published an influential book on this topic in 1962, *How to Do Things with Words*. One of Austin's favorite examples to demonstrate the pragmatic function was promises. When you make a promise you are not describing the world around you. You are creating an obligation and an expectation. To pronounce a marriage, declare war, christen a ship, renounce kin; these are all classic examples of the pragmatic function of language at work.

The anthropology of religion was important in developing our understanding of language pragmatics. Bronislaw Malinowski, an early pioneer of ethnographic fieldwork, wrote extensively about "the magical word" in *Coral Gardens and Their Magic* (1935), his study of traditional religion among the Trobriand Islanders of Melanesia. One of Malinowski's central findings was that "words in their primary and essential sense do, act, produce, and achieve" (1935: 52). He went even further when he wrote, "perhaps nothing demonstrates more clearly that words are acts and that they function as acts than the study of sacred utterances" (55). He discovered this through Trobrianders' use of "magical formulae" when they garden, to "produce fertility, ward off pests, guarantee the successful sprouting and growth of plants, make harvest plentiful and prevent yams from being eaten up too rapidly" (53). Trobriand garden magic cues us to the central role of language pragmatics in religion, but there are many other examples. In Muslim communities, reciting Qur'anic texts is a devotional act. In indigenous origin stories throughout the Americas, gods and spirits speak or sing the world into existence. And, for those who remember the 1973 film *The Exorcist*: "The power of Christ compels you!"

This section will also stress the way religious language makes extensive use of verbal art. Linguistic anthropologists define verbal art as stylized ways of speaking, in which a speaker must demonstrate performative competence to an audience. Verbal art is specialized speech, locally recognized as distinctive and socially powerful. Most forms of verbal art fit within a linguistic genre. Speech genres provide a framework for creating and consuming discursive acts. Genres vary by their use of select linguistic features. When performed in local contexts, religious language conforms to local expectations of what to say, when to say it, and how it should be said. This includes a wide range of stylistics: specialized vocabulary, patterned formulas, and poetic devices not common in everyday talk. Because verbal art is specialized, performers tend to be relatively few and socially prized. Verbal art produces verbal artists. This aligns very well with religious language because rituals tend to have ritual specialists. Divination needs a diviner, sermons need preachers, spells need witches, and prophecy needs a prophet.

Certainly, not all ritual speech is verbal art, but a great deal of it is. Prayer, the case study we explore first, exemplifies the verbal artistry of religious language. As we consider three examples of prayer, keep these two issues of language in front of you. How is the pragmatic function of language evident? How is performative competence achieved and evaluated?

PRAYER

Prayer is found in widely diverse religious cultures, not strictly the Abrahamic traditions of Christianity, Islam, and Judaism. Indeed, when it comes to religious language, we are hard pressed to think of a genre that is nearly as universal. Identifying prayer can be tricky. In different speech communities, prayer can overlap with several related genres: chants, spells, songs, divination, poetry, and others.

Moreover, prayer takes many forms. Prayer can be highly scripted, but also quite spontaneous. Prayer can be performed privately, in small groups, or in massive gatherings. Wherever it exists, prayer is about healing, both physical and spiritual. We begin our comparison of prayer in the southwestern United States.

The Navajo are an indigenous tribe, well known in anthropology as the most written about and photographed people in the world (Peterson 2013: 38n4). Navajo traditional religion is widely practiced, despite the fact that missionaries have been regular fixtures among the Navajo since the mid-1700s. Studies of ceremonial prayer are a good example of their "most written about" status; from Washington Matthews' "The Prayer of a Navajo Shaman" in 1888 to Gladys Reichard's *Prayer: The Compulsive Word* in 1944 and Sam Gill's *Sacred Words* in 1980. The discussion below is drawn from Margaret Field and Taft Blackhorse, Jr. (2002), who analyzed prayers recorded on Navajo reservation land during the 1940s.

Most Navajo ceremonial rituals address personal healing, such as calls for protection from evil spirits and exorcisms. These rituals can last anywhere from one to nine nights, and are led by a medicine man (*hataali*). Medicine men (and, less commonly, women) speak and sing prayers that are addressed directly to the deities. Most prayers conclude with four repetitions of the phrase *hozho nahasdlii* (harmony/ beauty has been renewed). Poetic devices, like repetition, help define the context as one of ritual healing.

Field and Blackhorse (2002) concentrate on the poetic device of parallelism in meaning rather than sound. An example of parallelism in sound would be rhyming or alliteration, but Navajo prayer does not do this. Instead, prayers include verbal patterns like the following, which forces illness out of the body: "Today from my toes it will radiate out (as a vapor), from the tip of my body it will radiate out, from the tips of my fingers it will radiate out, from the tips of my speech it will radiate out." Navajo prayers are not requests, but imperatives that "command and compel deities to act in a certain manner" (219). For this reason, ritual healers must precisely perform the formulaic language of prayer.

From the southwestern United States, we move to the Ecuadorean Andes. Quechua speakers throughout the Andes are Inca descendants, and Quichua refers to the Ecuadorian varieties. Like the Navajo, the Quichua have a long history of being missionized (primarily by Spanish Catholics). Anthropologist Rachel Corr (2004) studied a genre of prayer among a Quichua group that derives its name from the Spanish term for blessing (*bendicion*). In Corr's example, prayer involves code-switching between Spanish and Quichua and embeds formal Catholic prayers into traditional Quichua poetics. On the surface, this might look like a form of indigenous Catholicism, but in fact it is a "recentering" (Corr 2004: 383) of Catholic prayers. While it uses Catholic ritual speech, the focus remains on the Quichua verbal canon, indigenous aesthetics, and the traditional religious element of remembering the ancestors.

The main example Corr analyzes is a food blessing over a ceremonial meal, "Blessing of the Table." Textual elements from Catholic prayers (e.g., "this daily bread") are combined with features of traditional Quichua poetics (e.g., quoting ancestral words). The preferred ritual orators (*rezachij*, literally "prayer-makers") are elder Quichua men, as opposed to younger men. This is important because elders are more closely associated with traditional religion. Corr argues that this food blessing prayer is "an act of memory, linking [contemporary Quichua] with their collective genealogies" (398). Prayer becomes a way to tell the indigenous history that is excluded from official, state-sponsored histories. In turn, prayer is a form of resistance for the Quichua because it is "rooting the words within a collective ancestral past," not the dominant narrative of missionary colonialism.

From the Ecuadorian Andes, we move to Indonesia. John Bowen's *Muslims through Discourse* (1993) is an ethnography of the Islamic Gayo. The Gayo are an ethno-linguistic group who live in the western highlands of Sumatra. This region was under Dutch colonial rule from 1904 to 1945, but its Muslim history dates back to the 1600s. The heart of Bowen's analysis is the struggle and tension that occurs between "modernist" Muslims who seek to break completely with traditional Gayo religion and Muslims who are comfortable integrating Islam with traditional ritual practices.

Religious language is a major site of this tension. *Doa* is the local Gayo term for "any utterances directed to God or to spiritual agents" (Bowen 1993: 82). Bowen observes four types of *doa*: spells, requests, recitations, and prayers. Gayo prayer (*berdoa*) is distinguished from these other types in several ways. Prayer is directed only to God. Prayers can be spoken publicly or privately, but they differ linguistically. "Public prayer is entirely in Arabic" (83), while private prayer is in the Gayo language. Lastly, "prayers contain specific requests" (83). Because of this last feature, prayers are troublingly close to spells. Spells are part of the traditional Gayo religious repertoire (performed in three languages: Gayo, Arabic, and Indonesian), and they stress pragmatic effect. Bowen compares Gayo spells to the Trobriand garden speech documented by Malinowski. The rub for the Gayo is this: "modernist" Muslims deny "a direct causal link between an utterance and the receipt of a benefit" (80), stressing instead God's agency in responding to human requests. Prayer is still about healing for the Gayo, but it is not attributed the pragmatic power we see among the Navajo because of the complex distinctions made between the four types of *doa*.

LANGUAGE IDEOLOGIES

So far we've talked about religious language mainly in terms of one genre, prayer. Another important issue is the set of language ideologies that a speech community fosters. The term "language ideology" refers to beliefs and attitudes about language use and the nature of language itself. For example, consider the Gayo example we just examined. Why must public prayer be spoken in Arabic (and not Gayo or Indonesian)? Because Arabic is the language of the Qur'an, Muslims' holy scripture, it is understood to be the only appropriate way to speak directly to God or recite verses from the text. Most Muslims throughout the world share this language ideology. Religious identity, experience, and practice can be powerfully shaped by language ideologies. Two examples from Protestant Christian traditions will help demonstrate.

Anthropologists of Christianity have discovered a Protestant language ideology that emphasizes sincerity. Webb Keane (2002) describes this as the largely unquestioned assumption that words have a transparent relationship with beliefs: "sincere speech adds and subtracts nothing in words that was not already there in thought" (74). This model of the sincere speaker places a prime value on truth-telling, personal intention, individualism, and speech as a direct reflection of moral character, and favors spontaneity over rote formula. This model is consistent with other elements of Protestantism, such as the central necessity of truthful doctrine and the value of belief proclamations. In turn, this language ideology has a large stake in judgments of authentic faith.

Anthropologists of Christianity have also shown that this sincere speaker model can clash with the local language ideologies of convert populations. Joel Robbins (2001) details an example in his ethnography of the Urapmin, a society of less than 400 people living in the western highlands of Papua New Guinea who experienced a mass conversion to Pentecostal Christianity in the late 1970s. Unlike many convert populations, the Urapmin did not seek to integrate their newfound religious culture with their traditional one: "With very few exceptions, Urapmin today are strikingly uninterested in the possibility of syncretizing Christian and traditional ideas" (Robbins 2001: 903). However, they struggle mightily with prayer and other genres of Christian talk, which became "the most routine part of their religious practice" (904). Whereas the sincere speaker model requires a deep trust in spoken language, their traditional language ideology promotes a distrust of the spoken word. In traditional Urapmin thinking, "thoughts, feelings, and desires are hidden in the human heart [and] cannot be reliably communicated through speech" (906). Conversion for the Urapmin has been about much more than simply adopting new religious beliefs. Conversion has meant coming to terms with new ways of understanding the nature of words and what they can do.

For a second illustration, consider contrasting Christian ideologies about silence. Words mediate, but so does their absence. Richard Bauman (1974) studied worship practices among English Quakers from 1650 to 1690. Part of early Quaker theology was that the Bible "constituted a word of God … and that revelation was an ongoing and progressive process, to be realized by every man" (145). Individuals could directly experience divine revelation through their "Inner Light." This refers to a spiritual part of the human make-up "inaccessible to man's natural and earthly faculties" (145). "A suppression of the earthly self" (145) was required to experience revelation, which Quakers equated with being silent. Ritual silence allowed adherents to listen to their Inner Light. As a result, Quaker worship was defined by long stretches of silence, punctuated by Inner Light proclamations, and returns to silence. Theology was language ideology, namely a de-valuing of constant talking.

Compare this Quaker imperative toward ritual silence with a case of ritual failure. Over the course of 20 years Simon Coleman did ethnographic fieldwork with a charismatic Christian megachurch in Sweden. Coleman (2006) tells the story of one worship service where the preacher delivered an hour-long "breathless sprint through the Bible" (39). During the sermon, the preacher posed a question to the gathered crowd: "Have we never noticed the difference between a stillness that is empty and one that is full of God?" Typical worship services at this church concluded with an altar call, a rowdy mix of prayer, song, and speaking in tongues. Instead, the preacher closed this particular service by attempting to become the meaningful silence he had previously asked about by standing still and silent. This jolted the ecstatic mood, creating an incredible awkwardness. The worship service ended with a whimper, not the normal bang. Why? Coleman argues that this preacher's experiment failed because it ran afoul of charismatic communicative ideologies. The "ideal charismatic is both hearing and speaking, both receiving and broadcasting sacred language" (44). In the silence, the normal charismatic "exchange of language between persons [was] blocked" (57). Listeners were confused: to speak might challenge the preacher's authority, but to sit in devotional silence would reduce them to passive listeners. This is dramatically different than the high value Quakers place on silence. How would you describe the language ideologies—about words, speaking, and listening—that helps us distinguish the ritual lives of Quakers and charismatics?

Box 3.3 Religious words

In this section we highlighted three analytical tools for understanding the relationship between religious language and mediation:

- The pragmatic function: the ability of words to create, not just describe.
- Verbal art: stylized performances of speech genres, often done by ritual specialists.
- Language ideology: beliefs and attitudes about the nature of language, language use, speakers, and audiences.

If you are conducting research or fieldwork for your course, you can continue working with these concepts by applying them to your project. This works best if you have audio- or video-recorded data that can be analyzed closely. Alternatively, you can view one of the two films below, both of which are filled with rich examples of religious language:

- *Jesus Camp* (2006; 87 min.): portrait of a Pentecostal summer camp, profiling youth who attend and the leaders who organize the camp.
- *A Life Apart: Hasidism in America* (1997; 96 min.): portrait of the ultra-orthodox Hasidic Jewish community in Brooklyn, New York City.

Consider the following questions about the film on your own or with a course colleague:

- How many genres of religious language can you identify? What linguistic and performative features set each genre apart? What do we learn about speakers and their relationship with audiences?
- How is the pragmatic function of language evident across the genres you identified?
- What language ideologies are evident across the genres you identified?

THINGS

"Things" is a broad, vague, and playful term to use. Don't worry; we'll get specific, clear, and (mostly) serious. I mean for us to think about material objects and their role in religious mediation. In some traditions, material objects are the source of charged debate. Christianity is a great example. We could go back to the Byzantine Empire and the Iconoclastic Controversy of 700–900 CE, when the Church was bitterly divided over whether to venerate or destroy icons and images. Then again, in the 1500s, things were part of the schisms that divided the Protestant Reformation. Calvinism formed in opposition to Lutheranism in part because of "a flamboyant denial of the power of material things to mediate divine actions" (Keane 2007: 60). The Lutheran adherence to a Catholic Eucharist prompted John Calvin to accuse Luther of "a carnal and crass conception of God" (quoted in Keane 2007: 61). This history helps explain why some Christian churches today have elaborate architecture and artistry, while others are extremely austere in decoration.

But, troubling over things is by no means only a Christian concern. Consider the Afro-Caribbean traditional religion of the Garifuna, an indigenous, ethno-linguistic group now living in Honduras, Guatemala, Belize, and Nicaragua. Their ancestry is a mix of African and Amerindian groups who lived on the Caribbean island of St. Vincent in the 1600s. Difficult economic conditions in Central America combined with a liberalized U.S. immigration policy in 1965 to bring one third of the 300,000 Garifuna to the United States. In his ethnography, *Diaspora Conversions* (2007), Paul Johnson did fieldwork among Garifuna spirit possession shamans (*buyei*) in the homeland (rural Honduras) and in the diaspora (New York City).

Altars are a pivotal ritual element for Garifuna shamans. Altars are used to mediate relations with ancestral spirits and are filled with eclectic mixes of material objects. Understanding why certain objects are on the shamanic altar, and why some are not, goes a long way to understanding Garifuna religion. In Honduras, maracas and bottles of rum sit crowdedly next to pipes, cigars, sticks, pictures of Catholic saints, and other items. The stick is placed on the shaman's head to moderate possession trances. Pipes and maracas were part of the earliest explorer accounts of Carib Island religious practice. And, the saints were borrowed from missionaries and are now petitioned along with the ancestors for healing and curing.

Things matter across widely different religious traditions, from European Calvinists to Afro-Carib shamans. And, things serve many functions. They are vehicles of spiritual power, ritual aids, representations of the divine, and signifiers of religious history. They are present in ritual life and everyday life. We could take the broad topic of "things" in many directions, so it will be helpful to concentrate on one particular kind of material object: commodities.

COMMODITIES

Commodities are products bought, sold, and traded according to a market value. In capitalist contexts value is about economic cost, but it is also about the social life and significance of a commodity. Value can differ by how much sense a commodity makes to a consuming public, how many markets it circulates through, and how much excitement it generates. In global capitalist contexts, commodities undergo massive campaigns of advertising and branding.

Marxist scholars have a long tradition of studying commodities. We won't rehearse that tradition here, but it will help us to consider one of the most penetrating insights of Marxist scholarship: the process of commodification is not just about creating a market *of* things, it is about creating a desire *for* things. This insight segues into a question that preoccupies scholars of religion, as well as many religious adherents. How do religion and capitalist consumption work together? (Note how this recalibrates Weber's central question in *The Protestant Ethic and the "Spirit" of Capitalism* (1905), which emphasized capitalist production.)

In some ways, religion and capitalism could be seen as competing systems. They compete for time, energy, loyalty, wants, and needs. Yet, people find many ways to integrate commodity consumption into their religious lives. For example, we find Garifuna shamans decorating altars with purchased items. We also find the craft production and mass production of religious commodities, from Bibles to Buddha statues. In the three examples below, keep a close eye on how capitalist consumption works with religious ideals and ambitions. Do they fit together neatly or do they exist in tension with one another?

In her ethnography, *An Imagined Geography* (2004), JoAnn D'Alisera studied the social and religious lives of Sierra Leonean Muslims in Washington, D.C. In 1989, a civil war erupted in the West African nation of Liberia. This soon bled over into neighboring Sierra Leone, igniting an 11-year armed conflict. Thousands of Sierra Leonean refugees were displaced. In the D.C. diaspora, D'Alisera found that popular religious commodities played an important role in their everyday lives.

Bumper stickers, Qur'an recitation cassettes, educational pamphlets, prayer rugs, prayer beads, perfumes, oils, incense, bookmarks and key chains with Qur'anic script, alarm clocks and wristwatches that announce prayer times, coffee mugs, holiday cards, and postcards: all are sold at the D.C. Islamic Center. Most of D'Alisera's consultants held working-class jobs, such as men who drove taxis and women who operated street corner food stands. These men and women found versatile uses for popular Islamic commodities. Along with their devotional purpose, these migrants used commodities to "inscribe," to write on, everyday life with a sense of order. A Qur'anic key chain, something so small, linked them to the global Muslim community and helped calm "the burden of physical and cultural displacement" (2004: 80). Even more, because a place like the inside of a taxi cab is both private and public, religious commodities were a means of "making Muslim space" (78). This is no small feat, if we remember that this is a marginalized group several times over, and that claiming space is always an act of power.

From the streets of the U.S. nation's capital, we travel to the streets of Seoul, South Korea. There, Laurel Kendall (2008) did ethnographic research with Korean shamans who perform healing rites (*kut*) "for clients whose domestic troubles, business reverses, or ill health cause them to suspect, and to solicit a shaman's divination to confirm, that the ancestors are hungry and the gods want to play" (155). Through feasts and entertainment organized by the shaman, the spirits get satisfied and clients' worries are allayed. The feasting and entertaining of the *kut* makes ample use of food commodities.

The broader economic context is especially important in this example. Contemporary South Korea is a place of recent financial wealth. A military dictatorship from 1961 to 1987 that enforced austerity measures (e.g., rice rations) gave way to an economic boom, marked by global prestige (e.g., Seoul hosted the 1988 Summer Olympics) and conspicuous consumption. Many Koreans are morally torn about wealth and consumption: they like global prestige, but they remember austerity and worry about losing a national identity to global capitalism. This ambiguity reappears in the shamanic healing ritual. The spirits have more refined tastes compared to earlier generations. The *kut* now involves imported fruits like bananas, foreign whisky like Johnny Walker Red, and delicacies like boxes of chocolates (Kendall 2008: 154). Terms like "offerings" or "symbols" do not adequately capture this ritual use of commodities. They are more like "props." Like theatrical props that increase a performance's drama and believability, shamanic props increase ritual success.

For our third example, we shift methodological gears. *Toying with God* (2010) is a study in comparative religion by Nikki Bado-Fralick and Rebecca Sachs Norris. Their subject is a mass-produced global commodity: religious games and dolls. To name just a few artifacts they collected and analyzed: the marketplace of religious toys includes Hindu lunch boxes, board games like the Jewish *Kosherland*, dashboard Buddhist monks, Bible action figures, and Fulla dolls (the Muslim anti-Barbie).

We could argue that religious games and dolls serve several functions. They might help socialize children into a religious tradition. They might be a way to make leisure meaningful (rather than, say, sinful or wasteful). They might be an evangelistic strategy. They might even be a way to parody, satirize, or subvert one's own or another religious tradition. While not discounting these, *Toying with God* emphasizes another possibility. Religious games and dolls are an example of lived religion that mediates aspects of modern life we tend to separate: fun entertainment and serious religion, leisure and devotion, play and worship. In doing so, these commodities engage us as "embodied, sensing, feeling, thinking beings" (Bado-Fralick and Sachs Norris 2010: 96). And with this, we come full circle, back to the body's role in religious mediation.

Box 3.4 Religious materiality

On your own, or with class colleagues, reflect on the role of things in religious mediation. You might begin with the question we posed at the start of this section: How do religion and capitalist consumption work together? For the examples presented:

- How are commodities used in religious practice?
- Where did you see a comfortable fit?
- Where did you see tension?
- How did commodities suggest a permeable boundary between "religion" and other parts of social life?

You might also work with the following exercise. Search online for a company or place that sells religious commodities. (You might stick with one of this section's examples: find a religious toy company; or, find the Islamic Center of Washington D.C. website.)

- What range of religious commodities is being sold?
- How are they presented to consumers?
- How do they engage, or comment on, their religious tradition?
- How are they similar, or dissimilar, to the examples in this section?

CHAPTER SUMMARY

In this chapter, we explored the process of religious mediation. Individuals and local communities find ways to make the immaterial of religious life visible, tangible, visceral, and material. Beliefs are communicated, morals lived out, emotions expressed, and spirits manifest. The internal is externalized. The extra-human enters the realm of the very human. Mediation is a process that happens amid multiple social contexts: immediate ritual frames, local community life, regional politics, national economies, global flows, and historical tradition. For this exploration, we relied on a number of ethnographic guides:

- Two cases of soul food: African-American Sunni Muslims and the African Hebrew Israelites of Jerusalem.
- Three genres of evangelical Brazilian music: hip hop, gospel singing, and samba.
- The status of blood among Ethiopian Israelis and Mormons in the United States.
- Three examples of prayer: Navajo healers, Quichua ritual orators, and Gayo Muslims in Indonesia.
- Conflicting language ideologies among Urapmin Pentecostals of Papua New Guinea.

- Two cases of ritual silence: Quakers in England and charismatic Christians in Sweden.
- Three examples of commodity use: Sierra Leonean Muslims, Korean shamans, and religious toys.

To make sense of these examples, we relied on a series of concepts:

- mediation
- habitus
- language pragmatics
- verbal art
- language ideology
- commodification.

Ultimately, this chapter helps us think about the deeply social nature of religious life. This chapter also helps show us something of the physicality, tactility, and sensuousness of religion. I hope you have glimpsed the widely different ways religious mediation can happen. And, we have really only scratched the surface! If you are working on a research or fieldwork project for your class, what else are you glimpsing about mediation?

SUGGESTIONS FOR FURTHER READING

Along with the works cited in this chapter, consider these books and essays as productive next places to go. To follow up on "Mediation," there is a provocative exchange between Matthew Engelke and Charles Hirschkind in the journal *Social Anthropology* (2011, 19(1)), which exposes important theoretical issues in religious mediation. For "Bodies," a foundational essay for the anthropology of religion is Thomas Csordas' "Embodiment as a Paradigm for Anthropology" (*Ethos*, 1990). For an ethnography that links religion, the senses, and political power there is Charles Hirschkind's *The Ethical Soundscape: Cassette Sermons and Islamic Counterpublics* (Columbia University Press, 2006). To continue with "Words," a useful review essay is Webb Keane's "Language and Religion" (in *A Companion to Linguistic Anthropology*, Blackwell, 2004). For an ethnography that links religion, language, gender, and socialization there is Ayala Fader's *Mitzvah Girls: Bringing up the Next Generation of Hasidic Jews in Brooklyn*

(Princeton University Press, 2009). For "Things," an excellent resource is the edited volume, *Things: Religion and the Question of Materiality* (Fordham University Press, 2012), which gathers 22 theoretical, ethnographic, and historical essays. You may also enjoy exploring *Material Religion* (www.bloomsbury.com/us/journal/material-religion/), a top notch journal in the anthropology of religion and religious studies.

4

IN TIME, IN PLACE

The Beng are a relatively small society (c.12,000 people) living on the political and economic margins of the Ivory Coast in West Africa. They are Côte d'Ivoire's oldest indigenous group, and most Beng use traditional strategies of farming, hunting, and gathering to subsist. Amid increasing conversion to Christianity and Islam, many Beng continue to practice their traditional religion. A distinguishing feature of Beng religion is their claim that infant children lead profoundly emotional and spiritual lives. This is because Beng babies are not new people with no sense of self and no memory, they are reincarnations of an ancestor (Gottlieb 2004).

When a Beng baby is born he or she begins the transition into this world from *wrugbe* (literally, "spirit village"). *Wrugbe* is a space and time that exists between death and new life. It is the place of residence for all Beng who have not yet reincarnated. *Wrugbe* is a spiritual place with this-worldly coordinates. Beng adults locate *wrugbe* to be a series of invisible neighborhoods that are dispersed across major African and European cities. The home of dead ancestors and yet-to-be reincarnated children, *wrugbe* is accessible to Beng adults through dreams, to which they travel and return with stories to share (Gottlieb 2004).

Until a newborn's umbilical cord stump falls off, they are considered to still be completely in *wrugbe*. The Beng do not hold funerals for newborns who die; indeed, such passings are not considered deaths in local terms, simply the bodily return to *wrugbe* of a person who was not yet ready to come back to this world. When the umbilical stump does detach, the child begins a several-year journey to complete the separation from *wrugbe*. Because Beng babies are not simply born, but emerge from *wrugbe*, their status as fully spiritual persons has clear and distinct ramifications for child-rearing practices (Gottlieb 2004).

For example, parents "do all they can to make this life comfortable and attractive for their infant, to ensure that their child is not tempted to return to *wrugbe*" (Gottlieb 2004: 87), including gifts of cowrie shells (an important currency for the ancestors). As a gathering place for all who die, not only the Beng, *wrugbe* is an essentially multi-lingual place. Linguistic socialization is not a matter of children learning the Beng language, it is a matter of children losing all the other languages they learned from living in *wrugbe*. For this reason, Beng caretakers constantly involve infants as full participants in everyday conversation. Beng babies know full well what is being said around them. Beng mothers will apologize to and joke with their babies, speech acts that presume a culturally and linguistically competent listener. While they cannot yet speak because they have not fully separated from *wrugbe*, Beng infants have full linguistic comprehension just as they lead full spiritual lives. Unlike most Western models for infancy, Beng babies are not agent-less persons or blank canvases who have yet to gain any real identity. They are full of intention, memory, and a sense of self (Gottlieb 2004).

WORLD-MAKING

The spiritual life of a Beng baby illustrates how religions situate their adherents within a particular reality. Religions provide experiential, ideological, moral, social, and cosmological structures that adherents accept as true and definitive. To deconvert away from a particular religion involves a rejection of some or all of the tradition's reality structures. To move across religious worlds is very much a matter of moving across planes of reality. The concept of "religious worlds" is, then, a productive comparative category for the anthropology of religion. (Moreover, if religious worlds constitute different lived realities, then studying across religious worlds is an excellent exercise in cultural relativism, a pillar of anthropological thinking.)

The problem of how religious worlds are made is outlined in the work of William Paden (1988). Paden argues that religious systems are best thought of as worlds (or, realities) that require construction and constant maintenance. "Each religious community acts within the premises of its own universe, its own logic, its own answers to its own questions" (7). Paden's approach reiterates a critique we discussed in Chapter 1 of intellect-only definitions of religion. Rather than reduce religion to a set of beliefs, values, or doctrines, we should always see religious worlds as "something lived in, acted out, embodied" (57). The Beng demonstrate this perfectly. It is not simply that they have ideas about reincarnation, they organize the everyday care of infants according to *wrugbe*'s relationship with this world.

All religious worlds plot their adherents on the two horizons of time and place. Our discussion throughout this chapter is organized around these two axes of orientation, so it will be useful to outline some key aspects of each upfront. As part of the broader study of culture, anthropologists use the term "temporality" to refer to lived models for the nature of time and its passing (Guyer 2007). Religious worlds help establish this for their adherents, often defining the primary or only temporality that structures everyday life. Paden writes: "each religious world has its own past. Each has its own history" (1988: 75), and I would add its own present and future as well.

The temporality of religious worlds can provide adherents with explanations for the origins of life, what happens after individuals die, where the spirits reside, and the end of all existence. Religious worlds present possibilities like the Beng's endless cycle of reincarnation, Buddhists' nirvana as a break from their cycle of death and rebirth, and the promise of messianic return in numerous Christian and Jewish traditions. Some Protestant traditions divide history into periods they call "dispensations," which humanity is progressing through on the way to a new heaven and a new earth (Harding 2000). Paden writes that "religions are communities of memory more ·than they are collections of dogmas" (1988: 78). By stressing memory, he is stressing that religious worlds are not just ways of explaining how time unfolds. They are also ways for people to construct relationships with the past, in order to foster identity and organize religious life. This is why religious calendars feature devoted times of remembrance: Ramadan for Muslims, Jewish *shmita*, and festivals for the saints in Catholicism and Eastern Orthodoxy.

Place, like time, is a primary axis of orientation. *Senses of Place* (1996a) is a brilliant collection of anthropological essays edited by Steven Feld and Keith Basso. The focus of this volume is the human act of creating attachments to places. The editors describe these attachments as "local theories of dwelling—which is not just living in place but encompasses ways of fusing setting to situation, locality to life-world" (Feld and Basso 1996b: 8). Dwelling captures the fundamental difference between physical space and inhabited place. The latter is about the active and socially performed imposition of meaning onto spaces. A sense of place, like temporality, orients a religious world, gives it bearings. And, like temporality, senses of place are not merely about theories, beliefs, meaning, and values; they encompass fully embodied engagements with everyday life.

Claims of sacred space are one pivotal way in which sense of place is expressed by religious worlds. Religious scholars in the social sciences have established three models for understanding sacred space (Lane 2001). "Ontological" approaches view sacred space as "radically set apart from everything profane" (57). Spaces are thoroughly and definitively special, either sacred or not. This approach reifies the division between sacred and profane (see Chapter 1), a move that many would argue is a misreading of Durkheim. "Cultural" approaches shift the emphasis away from spaces being inherently sacred to viewing space as socially constructed. The human engagement with space is historically formed, collectively managed, and ideologically saturated. Methodologically, this creates an opportunity to see how spaces become invested with multiple meanings and the locus of competing claims to sacred space. "Phenomenological" approaches see space as socially constructed, but add to this a focus on how the "topography and material character" (58) of spaces structure possibilities for human experience. Here, there is a dynamic interaction between religious communities and places themselves.

Feld and Basso's "sense of place" is consistent with the cultural and phenomenological approaches, both of which are consistent with a Durkheimian stance that "locate[s] the sacred at the nexus of human practices and social projects" (Chidester and Linenthal 1995: 5). Religious communities invest spaces with sacred power and meaning, often because of the distinctive character of particular spaces. The production of sacred space occurs through "the human labor of consecration" and "the cultural labor of ritual, in specific historical situations, involving the hard work of attention, memory, design, construction, and control of place" (6). Cultural and phenomenological approaches recognize natural landscapes (e.g., Jewish claims to Israel–Palestine as their rightful biblical inheritance) and built environments (e.g., Mormon reverence for the Salt Lake Tabernacle) as sacred spaces.

It is also important to observe that time and place are not discrete world-making moorings, but are deeply entangled with one another. Models of temporality can imply special relationships with space, and senses of place can involve a temporal orientation. Again, the Beng illustrate a basic principle: *wrugbe* is a location in both time and space. We will encounter other ethnographic cases below, including the following two examples. Consider the creation stories of traditional Native American religions, which frequently involve the naming of particular sites on a local landscape as sacred. And, consider the practice of Christian pilgrimage to the "Holy Land" in Israel–Palestine, which is performed as a kind of oscillating time travel between biblical history and the present.

What are the everyday implications of living in a particular religious world? And, how do religious adherents accomplish and manage their projects of world-making? These are the questions we pursue in the remainder of this chapter. To do so, we examine different ways in which religious communities use ritual practices and narratives to construct and maintain models of temporality and senses of place. We begin with a very rich tradition of anthropological inquiry: the study of pilgrimage.

PILGRIMAGE

Individuals and groups perform devotional journeys to special sites as a kind of ritual travel in many religious traditions. The natures of pilgrimage sites are diverse. Some are integral to religious origins (e.g., Buddhist pilgrims to Lumbini, Nepal, where Siddhartha Gautama was born); some are sites of spiritual revelation (e.g., Tepeyac Hill in Mexico City, where the Virgin Mary appeared to Juan Diego); and some sites are reconstructions of historically important sites in a tradition (e.g., the replica of the Holy House of Nazareth in

Walsingham, England). In any case, thinking again with Emile Durkheim, sacredness is not simply discovered at pilgrimage sites, it is actively produced through every portion of the ritual journey (leaving home, traveling, arriving, devotion at the site, traveling back, and returning home). And, in any case, pilgrimage is a revealing ritual of religious world-making: for its function of producing the sacred, its attachment to place, and its experience of time. To further understand how pilgrimage engages the problem of religious world-making, we should consider how anthropologists have explained pilgrimage. There are three theoretical touchstones to consider.

COMMUNITAS

The first approach elaborates on a classic ritual theory. We owe this to Victor and Edith Turner's *Image and Pilgrimage in Christian Culture* (1978). The Turners argue that pilgrimage is a modern ("post-industrial" is their term) version of a rite of passage. This concept, rite of passage, derives from the work of French folklorist Arnold van Gennep (1909). van Gennep maintained that every society vene-rates certain ritual events, which function as public markers of status transformation. van Gennep argued that rites of passage contribute to social cohesion and reaffirm the established system of social roles. All rites of passage have three stages: separation, transition, and incorporation. As an example, consider the *hajj* (Islamic pilgrimage to Mecca, the city of Muhammad's birth and near the site of his first divine revelation, during the final month of the Islamic calendar).

Pilgrims separate themselves from their social peers, in part by traveling to this Saudi Arabian city but also by entering the ritual condition of *ihram* (this includes a wide range of hygiene practices and replacing everyday clothes with a seamless white garment). In the transitional stage, which van Gennep called liminality (from the Latin *limen* for "threshold"), ritual participants are betwixt and between their former status and their yet-to-be new status. Liminality is about being neither one nor the other, a time when social norms are suspended or reversed. During the *hajj*, this is most clearly evident in the way social leveling occurs through ritualization. From the uniform clothing to the fact that all pilgrims proceed through the same ritual practices in the same way, all worldly distinctions dissolve and everyone, irrespective of social position, are marked as equals during the ritual time. Finally, ritual participants are incorporated back into normal social life, with their change of status realized. Muslim pilgrims change out of their ritual clothing, many shave their heads as a visible sign of transformation, and return to their homes throughout the world as religiously different for having completed the journey. (For a good ethnographic sketch of this status change in a central Turkish village see Delaney (1990: 520)).

van Gennep and the Turners both stress liminality as the most crucial stage of the ritual process. The Turners argued that Christian pilgrimage was a post-industrial analogue ("liminoid"), because it is voluntary rather than built into any social structure as requisite. The Turners used the term *communitas* (Latin for "community") to describe the ritual condition achieved during the liminal phase. *Communitas* is defined by intense, intimate bonding among ritual participants; "a relational quality of full unmediated communication, even communion" (Turner and Turner 1978: 250). It captures both "a place and moment 'in and out of time'" (197). Rite of passage, change in status, experience of *communitas*: this is our first anthropological optic for explaining pilgrimage.

CONTESTATION

The second approach makes a sharp pivot, shifting away from a functionalist reading of social cohesion and the experiential unity emphasized by *communitas*. This approach, which we can call "contestation" (Coleman 2002a), is articulated clearly by an edited volume, *Contesting the Sacred: The Anthropology of Christian Pilgrimage* (Eade and Sallnow 1991). The contestation approach highlights two arguments. First, pilgrimage sites are social spaces where divergent groups, identities, and claims about the true nature of the site come into contact—often contentiously. Conflict and diversity, rather than the harmony of *communitas*, prevail. Second, pilgrims are not the only social actors involved in pilgrimage. There are also local residents, other travelers, business entrepreneurs, and site caretakers to account for. The relationships that form among these different actors, again often contentious, also shape rituals of pilgrimage. Consider an ethnographic example from Jerusalem.

Glenn Bowman (1991) shows how three Christian groups—Greek Orthodox (from Cyprus), Catholics (from England and Ireland), and evangelical Protestants (from the United States, South Africa, Great Britain, and the Netherlands)—interact differently with Jerusalem and its sites. Unlike the Islamic *hajj*, Christian pilgrimage is not obligatory and does not have a prescribed ritual itinerary. Bowman argues that this room for variation means that different Christian traditions will favor and neglect different pilgrimage practices, reflecting how Christianity has intra-religious differences.

Because materiality plays an important role for Eastern Orthodox Christians, pilgrims do things like "rush impatiently into the churches and proceed around the interiors kissing all the icons" (Bowman 1991: 110). And, given the centrality of the liturgical calendar, the experiential and theological apex for Orthodox pilgrims is to be "present in Jerusalem during the holy feasts" (111).

Catholic pilgrimage is "much more individuated," focused on the personal "revitalization of spiritual energies" not on "a cosmological celebration of the community of mankind in Christ" (113). Catholic and Orthodox Christians also diverge in how they engage the actual sites. Catholics distinguish "between the significance of the biblical events said to have happened at the sites and the places themselves" (114). The focus shifts from a physical space to a narrative about a place, thus rendering the act of being at a specific site unnecessary to achieve the desired spiritual experience. Orthodox Christians must be in exact locations, whereas for Catholics it is enough to just be in Jerusalem's Old City.

Evangelical Protestants perform yet a third version of Holy Land pilgrimage. For starters, the evangelical "desire to have an unmediated relation to the Bible" (116) creates a relative disinterest in Orthodox and Catholic churches, which represent "institutional domination rather than the truth which that institution has usurped and distorted" (ibid.). Evangelical pilgrims are far more likely to seek out the Garden Tomb (just beyond the Old City walls) rather than the Church of the Holy Sepulchre, and more likely to have profoundly spiritual experiences in the Garden of Gethsemane.

While all three Christian groups go to Jerusalem so that they can be "involved in the divine redemptive project" (119), they do so quite differently through their respective pilgrimages. Rather than "a holy city," Bowman encourages us to see "a *multitude* of holy cities ... built over the same spot, operating at the same moment, and contending for hegemony" (98). There are many Jerusalems, not one. (Of course, this is further compounded when we remember that Jerusalem is also a city of sacred spaces for Jews, Muslims, and secular historians!)

INTERSECTING JOURNEYS

Our third approach to pilgrimage pivots again, to what we might call "intersecting journeys" (Coleman 2002a; Badone and Roseman 2004). *Communitas* and contestation both focus on pilgrimage as religious ritual, composed of meaningful intentions, practices, and experiences. The intersecting journeys approach maintains an interest in ritualization, but widens the ethnographic scope to envision pilgrimage as one version of a broader type: sacred travel. In this approach, other forms of modern mobility are also about producing the sacred; for example, heritage tourism in which travelers seek personal, familial, and cultural roots (Ebron 2000). (Recall Chapter 1's discussion of "religion beyond 'religions,'" and the religious aspects of the seemingly non-religious.) Structurally, pilgrimage "overlaps with tourism, trade, migration, expressions of nationalism, creations of diasporas, [and] imagining communities" (Coleman 2002a: 363). In turn, a robust anthropology of pilgrimage should account for this convergence with other forms of sacred travel. Consider an ethnographic example from Kyoto, Japan.

Nelson Graburn (2004) analyzed a three-year conflict between the city of Kyoto and a local Buddhist Association. Kyoto attracts tens of millions of visitors each year. A major reason people travel there is to see the city's 1,700 Buddhist temples and 270 Shinto shrines. City officials and the Buddhist Association disagreed about whether there should be a required tax on revenue collected from entrance fees into temples and shrines. The city saw an opportunity to fund the maintenance and restoration of its historic buildings without endangering the operating budget. The Buddhist Association, representing 1,100 of the temples, claimed that religious institutions serving worshippers should not be subject to any such tax. Were travelers to the city's temples and shrines tourists or pilgrims? In this Kyoto conflict, the economic stakes of that question were quite high.

Graburn unravels this knot of disagreement by making some ethnographic observations. First, Japanese religious pluralism is not an either/or case in which people affiliate with either Buddhism or

Shinto. Rather, both are practiced in everyday contexts. Of the c.130 million Japanese, almost all are Shinto and most are Buddhist too. As a result, it is quite difficult to discretely sort Buddhist from Shinto pilgrims. Second, the Japanese language distinguishes among multiple forms of travel: *ryoko* (any kind of journey), *tabi* (a purposeful journey), *kanko/kenbutsu* (sightseeing), *henro/junrei* (a journey with specifically religious connotation), and *mairi* (visiting a religious site, but not necessarily for a religious purpose) (Graburn 2004: 132). In short, the linguistic stage is set for the city and the Buddhist Association to clash over what kind of traveler is there to visit the temples and shrines. Third, all Japanese pilgrimage includes features of modern tourism, and Japanese tourism "is rarely completely bereft of 'religious' practices" (132). This means that it is against the grain of local culture to strictly separate tourists from pilgrims.

Graburn's case study is instructive because it highlights the need to be thoroughly ethnographic in our understanding of tourism and pilgrimage as intersecting journeys. Claims of being a tourist *or a* pilgrim, of serving tourists *or* pilgrims, and of needing to separate tourists *from* pilgrims has consequential stakes, and different stakes depending on who you are in this cultural puzzle. Moreover, Graburn cautions us to be on guard against ethnocentrism, of using categories (e.g., *communitas*) derived only from studying Christian pilgrimage to understand Buddhist–Shinto pilgrimage.

Box 4.1 Explaining pilgrimage

Pilgrimage provides a fascinating avenue into the religious worlds that people inhabit, particularly because it foregrounds both spatial and temporal orientation. In this section, we discussed three anthropological frameworks for explaining pilgrimage: *communitas*, contestation, and intersecting journeys. Use these approaches to analyze another case study.

Diabla Blanca (2012; 60 min.) is a documentary about Japanese youth who travel to Mexico to participate in the annual pilgrimage of the Huichol Indians. You can view the documentary here: www.youtube.com/watch?v=GeYAEX qaPQg. (If you are unfamiliar with the Huichol, you can view a 30-minute primer about their pilgrimage here: www.

youtube.com/watch?v=bLz5yj3rAl0.) On your own, or with class colleagues, consider a few questions:

- How adequately does each framework explain the journeys of the Japanese youth and the Huichol? Are there ways in which these frameworks complement or compete with each other?
- What role do models of temporality play in these journeys? How do these journeys involve a sense of place? And, what do we learn about religious world-making given the cross-cultural nature of this encounter?
- Read alongside the other examples in this section, would you argue that pilgrimage is a universally applicable category? Or, do the cultural differences exceed what a single category can handle (i.e., calling them all "pilgrimage" does not benefit us)? Why/why not?

(You might return to this Box after reading Chapter 6, which outlines some anthropological tools for studying religious globalization and transnationalism.)

COMMUNITIES OF MEMORY

Remembering is a thoroughly religious act of world-making. It can be a way to define the past (temporality) and strengthen attachments to space (sense of place). Memory is affectively powerful and a galvanizing force for social action. Pilgrimage is one expression of this; Muslim and Christian pilgrims remember their founding prophets by visiting sites of birth and revelation. In this section, we explore four ethnographic case studies. As you read, ask what each example suggests about the role of collective memory in making and maintaining religious worlds.

GARIFUNA SHAMANS IN HONDURAS AND NEW YORK CITY

Our first example returns us to an ethnographic context introduced in Chapter 3: Paul Johnson's research with Garifuna shamans in rural Honduras and New York City (2007). In Chapter 3 we examined the materiality of the shamans' healing altars. Here, we consider the role of place and time in Garifuna collective memory. Paden's theoretical description of religious worlds as "communities of memory" resonates closely with Johnson's ethnographic depiction: "Shamans are ... keepers of memory" (2007: 104) who "link memory to the transcendent, inscrutable authority of the ancestors and therefore wield extraordinary influence" (105). However, collective memory operates differently in the homeland of Honduras and the migrant diaspora of New York City.

In Honduras, the spiritual labor of shamans is directed to the Caribbean island of St. Vincent. This is where the Garifuna were displaced by the British navy in 1797, and is remembered in Honduras as both the ancestral homeland and the place from which ancestors return to possess the shamans. Honduran altars reflect this attachment to St. Vincent, featuring small boats and hammocks that "call to mind the golden age on St. Vincent prior to the deportation as well as the journey itself" (113). Memory has also become a resource for maintaining traditional shamanic religion amid the increasing presence of Christian evangelists. Missionaries stress conversion, and therefore a rupture with the ancestral past, "consistently invok[ing] biblical passages to justify looking ahead instead of to the past" (119). In turn, shamans revere the past by giving ultimate authority to the ancestor spirits. The integration of time and place is also evident in this missionizing encounter: "Because the *cristianos* [Protestants] envision the future as both a time and a process involving the physical transformation of the village, their war against traditionalists is also one of space" (121).

Shamans in New York City expand the traditional Garifuna cosmology by including the broader African diaspora. They continue to see Honduras as a powerful spiritual home, but also plot themselves as "part of a specific religious family that includes Santeria, Palo Monte, Vodou, Candomble, and Spiritism" (125). When diaspora shamans narrate their identity they stress a new consciousness gained from living in New York City. They are now awakened to their African roots, which "has both the general effect of giving value to an African genealogy that was forgotten, neglected, or suppressed and specific effects on the way given symbols are viewed" (133). Again, this is evident through the materiality of religious life. New York shamans use ritual herbs and jewelry (necklaces and bracelets) that overtly incorporate the Yoruban pantheon and various Afro-Carib spirits. Altars are "replete with objects familiar to students of West African-influenced religions in the Americas" (136), including the effectual instruments of Vodou, like scissors to "cut and reverse a particular set of difficult circumstances" (138). In contrast, African-originating spirits were never part of homeland shamans' religious practice.

Ultimately, differences in religious memory were one way for Johnson to distinguish between homeland and diasporic religion. Honduran shamans cultivated a remembrance of St. Vincent, whereas diaspora shamans looked to Africa as well as Central America. Johnson's ethnography illustrates very well how temporality and sense of place are mutually informed.

CHRISTIANITY IN THE U.S. SOUTH

The tight coupling of religious memory and sense of place is also a theme in the ethnography of southern U.S. Christianity. Consider two examples. Sascha Goluboff (2011) writes about the deeply emotional character of attachments to home among rural African-Americans in Virginia's Shenandoah Valley. Bradd Shore (2008) writes about narratives of family and spiritual renewal at an annual camp meeting 40 miles east of Atlanta, Georgia.

Goluboff's ethnography details a small African-American Methodist church (c.30 members), founded in 1869, whose members are direct descendants of local slaves. Living in a white majority town, "home church" and "homeplace" have a special valence due to the racist legacies of slavery, Jim Crow, and post-Civil-Rights discrimination. For these residents, home is the place of both bondage and freedom. In turn, their attachment to space produces "contradictory emotions of love, fear, and loyalty" (372). Goluboff's primary argument is that this sense of home "influences the faith journeys of individual congregants within the emotional repertoires of the family" (375). She illustrates this through narratives of early ritual socialization within the female line: "through worship, prayer, singing, and Bible study, mothers, aunts, and grandmothers built the foundation of the younger generation's faith" (379). She also records narratives of homecoming, in which adults return to the place of their youth to be "caretakers of others, like their kinswomen had done, and as such, they needed the guidance of Jesus through prayer and church fellowship to help them cope" (382).

Shore's ethnography takes us to a Methodist-founded camp meeting. The site itself covers over 100 acres with buildings dating as far back as 1840. Families return to the camp for one week every summer to share dedicated family time and religious worship. His primary argument is that this experience of ritual retreat combines "spiritual revival and family revival," primarily through "intense memory work" (2008: 101). The camp's daily schedule is "a relatively relaxed day of family time on the porches punctuated by bible classes and church services" (106). Campers ground this schedule in a collective nostalgia for an imagined past, which also serves as a critique of the present: "This [simplicity] contrasts markedly with the time trends of modern life that feature 'time famine,' fragmented schedules and considerable multitasking" (ibid.). Shore collected individuals' narratives about returning to the camp year after year. In their stories, participants recall a range of multi-sensory memories. For example, they recall the seeming omnipresence of sawdust on tent and sanctuary floors. Memory and materiality mingle: some participants mail sawdust to relatives who can't make it one summer and others request to have camp sawdust mixed with their burial ashes (109).

MESCALERO APACHE

For a final example of how collective memory fuels religious world-making, we can turn to a classic subject in anthropology: indigenous creation stories. Sometimes called "base narratives" or "origin myths," ethnographers in every generation have listened to, recorded, translated, and collected indigenous accounts of how the world began, where people come from, the nature of life, and the organization of the cosmos. Of course, we should remember that even though such narratives can be collected, they are not museum objects. They are an ongoing piece of social life, a resource indigenous peoples use to suture past to present to future. Consider an example from native North America.

Claire Farrer's *Thunder Rides a Black Horse* (1994) is an ethnography set on the Mescalero Apache reservation in south-central New Mexico. Farrer focuses on the four-day, four-night puberty ceremony;

a rite of passage held every summer in which young girls become women. The ceremony takes months and much energy to prepare and is the focal point of the community while it is happening. It is strenuous for the ceremonial girls. On Days One and Four they are "involved in intensive rituals throughout the morning and night" (Farrer 1994: 55), primarily dancing. The structure of the ceremony retells the Mescalero creation myth, which explains that the world was made in four days. The ceremonial girls ritually assume the role of White Painted Woman, the first woman told of in the creation story, and by doing so these girls transition into the role of adult female.

Farrer's central argument is that the Mescalero world is held together by a sense of "the mythic present," in which "the Long Ago and the Now are present together in thought, song, narrative, everyday life, and certainly in religious and ritual life" (2). The coming of age ceremony exemplifies this because it tethers each new generation of Mescalero girls to the Mescalero base narrative. As a ritual of remembrance, the girls' puberty ceremony recreates Mescalero cosmology, restates the social order, and reaffirms tribal attachments to the land.

(You can read a version of the Mescalero creation story online, curated by the University of Virginia. This particular performance was collected and published in 1938: http://xtf.lib.virginia.edu/xtf/view?docId=Apache/uvaGenText/tei/Mes05.xml&chunk.id=MN5&toc.id=MN5&brand=default.)

Box 4.2 Communities of expectation

Like memory, anticipation and expectation are expressions of temporality. And, just as they are communities of memory, religious worlds can also be organized around the future. Few do so more vividly, or with as much political and economic power, as evangelical Christians committed to a theology of apocalyptic End Times and messianic return. Consider the *Left Behind* book series, a fictional retelling of the New Testament Book of Revelation. The 16 volumes published between 1995 and 2007 have sold over 60 million copies in at least 37 countries and 33 languages. It is the highest grossing series in evangelical print history (Monahan 2008)!

This apocalyptic esprit is well-documented by Susan Harding in her historical ethnography, *The Book of Jerry Falwell* (2000). Harding demonstrates how this theology is not only a matter of belief, but a potent motivating and interpretive force in the lives of believers. She gives two prominent examples. Because the establishment of the nation of Israel and the rebuilding of the Jewish Temple are necessary preconditions for the Second Coming, adherents join Israeli Zionists in rejecting any Palestinian claim to the land. This has direct political consequences. Fundamentalists elect U.S. Congressional representatives and Presidents who formulate and enact various kinds of pro-Israeli policy. Harding also describes how "apocalypticism [is] ... a specific narrative mode of reading history; Christians for whom Bible prophecy is true do not inhabit the same historical landscape as nonbelievers" (2000: 232). Fundamentalists marshal interpretive strategies to discern what events are signs of the End Times, and use these strategies in their consumption of news media, evaluation of popular culture, and reactions to minor and major happenings at home and abroad.

While Harding's fieldwork concluded in the 1990s, Christian apocalypticism continues to produce End-Times-oriented institutions. On your own, or with class colleagues, analyze one such example: "Off the Grid News." This organization describes itself as "a fiercely independent, weekly email newsletter and website that is crammed full of practical information on living and surviving today and in future times when life may not be as easy." Its name derives from a desire to separate from mainstream commodities and infrastructures (e.g., food and energy) in order to prepare for when these resources fail and/or are depleted. Off the Grid News is owned and managed by evangelical Christians who exemplify Harding's "specific narrative mode of reading history." You might start with the first link below, then proceed to other stories on the site. Begin by reading five texts (you may want to collect more later), then address the questions below:

- www.offthegridnews.com/2013/10/10/bachmann-were-living-in-the-worlds-last-days/

- What model of temporality is being promoted by Off-the-Grid-ers? What relationship do they cultivate to the past, present, and future?
- What sense of place is produced as part of this Off the Grid temporality?
- How does Off the Grid illustrate the intimate link between beliefs and everyday practices?

CONTESTED PLACES

Attachments to place clearly play a crucial role in religious world-making. Religious communities foster historic and deeply affective relationships with land, particular sites, built environments, and political entities like cities. An issue we have yet to consider closely is that these relationships can emerge amid intense social, political, and religious conflict. Unlike time, places have an undeniable physicality. Because of this, many places experience competing claims to authentic belonging and ownership. Religious places are no exception and can exemplify the dynamics of inclusion and exclusion. We have glimpsed this briefly in a few examples already: Jerusalem's multiple residents and visitors, the clash between Protestant missionaries and Garifuna shamans, and discord between Japanese city officials and Buddhist monks. In this section, we elaborate on the contested dynamics of religious places in four ethnographic contexts. As you read each, keep a few questions in mind: Who has what at stake in contests over religious places? What do we learn about religious identity and world-making from contests over place? And, how are religious places embroiled in broader projects of contestation?

Our first case study of Tibetan Buddhists in China comes from Charlene Makley's ethnography, *The Violence of Liberation* (2007). Makley's fieldwork takes us to Labrang in central China (south-western Gansu Province), which is home to one of the six great Tibetan Buddhist monasteries, built in 1709. Tibetans live here amid the broader conflict between the Chinese state and the western region of Tibet. Tibet declared its independence in 1913, but was forcibly annexed back into the Chinese state in 1950. The effects of this conflict, along with the Chinese Civil War, impacted Labrang when the Chinese communist army occupied the town in 1949. Tibetan Buddhists were targeted as outsiders: monastic buildings were torched, Buddha statues dragged through the streets, and celibate monks forced to marry.

The Chinese state continued to encroach on Buddhist sacred space by building a major highway directly through monastic grounds, dividing the holy complex and opening it to various secular travelers. In the 1980s post-Maoist reforms were implemented, easing pressure on Tibetans' ethnic and religious presence. Labrang remained a powerful sacred site for Tibetans and reopened in 1981 as a university that trains aspiring monks. The combination of direct highway transportation, economic liberalization, and active monastic life produced a surge in tourist interest in Labrang, which then produced market businesses seeking profit from the tourist stream.

This is the context for Makley's research, which explores the gender dynamics of Tibetan Buddhist revival. In one example, she focuses on the ritual of circumambulation (in which worshippers take devotional walks around the Labrang monastery). Clerical and lay Buddhists perform the rite to gain karmic merit. (Many adhere to a "circumambulation standard" (Makley 2007: 164) of 10,000 circuits, which takes several years of walking several hours a day to complete.) Increasing numbers of monastic residents and pilgrims have made this ritual a strikingly visible part of Labrang's everyday life. The number of secular tourists is also increasing, some seeking Labrang as a destination and others passing through on the state highway. The result is tense, in which a religious and ethnic minority must play host to a continuous flow of interlopers.

Our second case returns us to the famously contested Holy Land and the ethnographic work of Glenn Bowman (1993). The co-presence of Jews, Christians, and Muslims in Jerusalem and its surrounding areas gives rise to many potent situations. Bowman details one such example: a "nearly inoperative" (1993: 434) Greek Orthodox monastery in the West Bank, on the road between Jerusalem and Bethlehem, just across the Israeli border. Amid the ever-volatile context of Israel–Palestine, Christian and Muslims visitors to this site manage an uneasy co-existence.

The sixth century monastery is claimed (mostly by Christians) to be built on the site where the Old Testament prophet Elijah rested after fleeing from the persecution of Jezebel, described in 1 Kings

19. Every July, for the week of St. Elijah's Feast day, Orthodox pilgrims come to the shrine. Their primary ritual act is "to place a chain attached to the wall of the church around their necks, kiss it three times and step through it" (434). The chain was discovered in a cave beneath the monastery and while some "local people see the chain as one which had bound the saint," others believe it "had bound Christians during Muslim persecutions" (ibid.). Local Muslims say different. They believe the chain to have healing power (its lineage unknown and mostly unimportant), and also seek it in order to cure "illness, bad luck, sinfulness, and even the evil eye" (435). Because the church opens for the Orthodox Feast day, this is a perfect time to make use of the healing chain. That it is a special day on the Orthodox calendar is of no consequence to Muslim visitors. In addition, there are plenty of local Palestinians, Christians and Muslims, who use gatherings at the site for social purposes (e.g., to eat with friends or spend a day with family).

Bowman argues that this confluence of purposes and identities works because the differences are mostly muted.

> Each individual was able to attribute to the place and the gathering meanings personal to them, and yet, because the time and the place served as a place of inscription for so many diverse meanings and motives, the feast constituted a community. People recognized that community at the same time as they recognized the multiplexity of its character; it was, in a very real sense, a concentration of the community which they moved through day to day but in a more dilute form. The only people excluded from this sensed community were those who would make rigorous the criteria of participation.
>
> (438)

The only people who fit this last description were Orthodox priests in charge of the Feast day and Palestinian nationalists who saw religious ritual as secondary to political presence. One lesson of this example is that contested places are not always necessarily contentious places.

Of course, given the right mixture, contestation and contention can mingle quite fiercely. Such an example comes from the anthropologist Radhika Subramaniam (1999) and her research on Hindu–Muslim violence in India. Her analysis tracks a series of conflicts that occurred in the early 1990s and how they are remembered. On December 6, 1992, a police barricade was over-run and a mosque was destroyed in northeast India. All involved were Hindutva: adherents of a fundamentalist, nationalist move-ment who claim India as a Hindu-only state and have a long history of demonizing Muslims as invaders. They destroyed the Islamic site in order to build a temple for worship, claiming the mosque was built atop the sacred birthplace of Rama (a highly revered avatar of the Hindu god Vishnu). The next day in Bombay, nearly 1,000 miles to the southwest, street riots erupted between Hindus and Muslims and lasted for several days. Just over a year later, a second series of riots erupted in Bombay with Hindu nationalists targeting Muslim citizens.

Subramaniam conducted fieldwork in Bombay several years later. She collected narratives of what happened during those three moments of unrest. She unearthed various explanations (some political, some economic, some caste-oriented), but most connected the riots to the destruction of the mosque in the north. Subramaniam argues that this ever-present tension between funda-mentalist Hindus and Indian Muslims produces a "culture of suspicion," which is "a fine interpretive web that snags the stray observation, the fragment of a story, the disturbing smell, or unusual sounds" (1999: 101).

Throughout the narratives she collects, no memory seems to be able to escape or detach itself from this culture of suspicion. For example, even non-fundamentalist Hindus reproduced Hindutva antagonisms by linking the riots to Muslim spatial and aural uses of public settings (street processions and daily calls to prayer). This culture of suspicion also involved "the constant marking of differ-ence in small yet significantly visible ways" (106). In one example, a Muslim consultant explained to Subramaniam that in the wake of the riots he stopped carrying his normal Urdu language newspaper in favor of a Hindi or Marathi language newspaper. As in many multi-lingual urban settings, the newspaper you read marks your social identity, belonging, and status. In India, only Muslims read the Urdu paper.

In short, religious violence emerging from an ongoing conflict over spatial and national belonging creates an unavoidable, per-meating mood that surrounds everyday encounters. This example also shows us how collective memory can stitch together contested places if there is a shared context of political and territorial dispute, even when they are separated by nearly 1,000 miles. (Note the parallel here with the "narrative mode of reading history" (Harding 2000: 232) among fundamentalist Christians. Both can and do bend any everyday event to a particular interpretive scheme.)

In our first three examples, places are contested between religion and the state and between different religious traditions. Struggles over place can also occur within the same religious tradition. This is demonstrated in our final example: Northern Ireland's political–ethnic–religious conflict. Since it was established as a province of the United Kingdom in 1921, Northern Ireland has been the site of political discontent. Certain factions desire an independent, sovereign nation-state, separate from Scotland, England, and Wales, while others wish to remain part of the United Kingdom. Beginning in the late 1960s discontent escalated. A period known as "The Troubles" endured for three decades, with a death toll of more than 3,000. Successive peace agreements in 1998 and 2006 stemmed the civil war, but separatism and sporadic violence persist. The conflict is organized by a division between two groups: a slight majority of British unionists and a large minority who wish to secede from the United Kingdom and form a united Ireland. The British loyalists (led by a fraternal group, The Orange Order) are deeply committed Protestants and Irish republicans are Roman Catholic.

For nearly a decade, Liam Murphy (2009) conducted ethnographic work in Northern Ireland, focusing on these competing and intersecting claims of national and Christian identity. Already a complicated case, Murphy introduces yet another wrinkle: the recent rise of charismatic Christians who promote a unified Northern Ireland grounded in a shared Christianity (both Catholic and Protestant). The charismatic community is politically and denominationally diverse, a striking fact because the Protestant–Catholic divide is severe and social segregation ensues from political identity. A key discovery of Murphy's ethnography is that Orange Protestants and charismatics use scripture differently in public spaces.

Murphy notes that "parading is a centuries-old cultural practice in Ireland that is used primarily, though not exclusively, by fraternal

Protestant organizations" (2009: 25). The Orange Order uses this social institution to symbolically and physically challenge the legitimacy of Catholic republicans. Every July, at least through the late 1990s, Orange members and supporters paraded "through an exclusively Catholic residential district" (13). And, every year, police barricades attempted to separate the Orange paraders from Catholic protesters: some years the encounter was limited to yelling, other years violence spilled over. In these processions the Orange paraders carry "symbol-laden objects and trappings" (14) replete with Old Testament references to being God's chosen people who are under threat from God's enemies. The "Christian motifs that appear in association with these parades include murals, hand-held placards, and occasionally more direct representations of unity between Protestant Ulster and Israel" (14).

Northern Irish charismatics also "represent identity in and through acts of movement that involve walking or parading through contested spaces" (25). They too rely heavily on biblical language and symbols. But, their scriptural focus shifts from the Old Testament to New Testament themes of healing. Spiritual and physical healing are pillars of charismatic Christianity, and in the Northern Irish context it is a healing of both individuals and the nation. Charismatics exhort loyalists and republicans alike for "having disregarded a clear Apostolic call to spirituality in favor of sectarianism, ungodliness, and illegitimate pride in their own institutions at the expense of God's will to move toward one another" (19). They emphasize that Catholics and Protestants share a common religious heritage that should be elevated above nationalistic fervor.

> This assertion of a common past may seem self-evident, until one recalls that for loyalists and republicans history is not read as a unity but from sharply different vantages: [loyalists] seeing theirs as the True Faith under siege by those who would impose papal tyranny and political oppression, [republicans] seeing their past as one of bitter disenfranchisement and discrimination by colonial authority.
>
> (22)

Here, charismatics use temporality to frame their claim to Northern Ireland's contested public spaces.

Box 4.3 Sacred space at 11,500 feet

The San Francisco Peaks are a mountain range in northern Arizona, near the city of Flagstaff. In 1938, the U.S. Forest Service agreed to let the state of Arizona develop a ski resort on the western slopes of the summit, Humphreys Peak. The Arizona Snowbowl is one of the state's most popular tourist destinations. However, the Snowbowl is also a point of contention with Navajo Indians, for whom the San Francisco Peaks are one of four sacred mountains (*Dook'o'oo'sliid*) described in the Navajo creation story. The Peaks are said to be a living being, harmed by human intrusions, and home to healing medicines and deities of Navajo cosmology (Dunstan 2010). (You can read a version of the Navajo creation story here: www-bcf.usc.edu/~lapahie/Creation.html.)

Because the Peaks sit 30 miles beyond the contemporary Navajo Nation reservation border (established between 1868 and 1934), the Navajo must make their legal protests on the grounds that their religious freedom is being infringed upon. They tried this in 1979, when the Snowbowl announced a plan to expand the resort. The tribe lost the court case (*Wilson v. Block 1983*). They protested again in 2002 under the American Indian Religious Freedom Act after another set of expansion plans were announced. This expansion included a proposal to produce artificial snow using "reclaimed water" (i.e., treated sewage water). Despite an initial court victory, the tribe again lost the case (*Navajo Nation v. U.S. Forest Service 2008*).

Navajo and inter-tribal protests of the Arizona Snowbowl continue. On your own, or with course colleagues, explore two websites that support native claims to sacred space:

- www.truesnow.org/
- www.sacredland.org/san-francisco-peaks/
- Listening to these native voices, what is the nature of their sacred space? What is the nature of endangerments to the Peaks? What cultural resources are being marshaled to defend the Peaks? How are their claims to sacred space grounded in temporality?

- To extend this analysis, you might locate articles for and against native claims in Flagstaff's major newspaper, *The Arizona Daily Sun*: http://azdailysun.com/. How do native voices and critics engage the debate around this contested place in the public forum of a newspaper?

CHAPTER SUMMARY

In this chapter, we have explored the problem of religious world-making. Religions provide an experiential, ideological, moral, social, and cosmological reality that adherents accept as true. Models of temporality and senses of place are essential for establishing this reality. Whether it is a matter of placing a community in history or defining sacred space, these axes are crucial for religious adherents as they engage the social processes of constructing, maintaining, challenging, and defending their religious world.

Being in time and in place is certainly about a cosmological orientation, as we saw with the spiritual lives of Beng babies. But, it is also about generating religiously significant practices. Pilgrimage as a rite of passage is a definitive example. We considered three anthropological explanations for pilgrimage: *communitas* (which we saw with the Islamic *hajj*); contestation (which we saw with three Christian identities in Jerusalem); and, intersecting journeys (which we saw with pilgrimage–tourism debates in Kyoto). Being in time and place also highlights how religious communities are communities of memory, which we saw through four ethnographic examples: Garifuna shamans, two cases of religious remembering in the U.S. south, and the mythic present among the Mescalero Apache. Finally, being in time and in place reveals how religious world-making can occur through divergent claims to dwelling and authentic belonging. We examined four ethnographic cases of contested places: Tibetan Buddhists in China; Christians and Muslims at a shared site in Israel–Palestine; Hindu–Muslim violence in India; and, competing Christianities in Northern Ireland.

Ultimately, I hope this chapter has demonstrated how the making of religious worlds is a social process with high stakes, and an ongoing process that is open to contestation. As you continue through the next two chapters, reflect on this book as a whole, read other anthropological case studies, and conduct your own religious ethnography, I hope you will keep your eye on time and place as pivotal world-making resources.

SUGGESTIONS FOR FURTHER READING

Along with the works cited in this chapter, consider these books and essays as productive next places to go. To follow up on "World-making," a volume edited by S. Brent Plate extends the concept of religious worlds to how religion and film are connected cross-culturally, *Representing Religion in World Cinema: Filmmaking, Mythmaking, Culture Making* (Palgrave Macmillan, 2003). For "Pilgrimage," the volume edited by Jill Dubisch and Michael Winkelman, *Pilgrimage and Healing* (University of Arizona Press, 2005) features 11 anthropological essays from diverse religious traditions and cultural settings. To continue with "Communities of memory," there is Michael Lambek's ethnography of collective remembering in Madagascar, *The Weight of the Past* (Palgrave Macmillan, 2002). For "Contested places," Glenn Bowman's edited volume—*Sharing the Sacra: The Politics and Pragmatics of Inter-Communal Relations around Holy Places* (Berghahn, 2012)— gathers 10 anthropological essays that explore the dynamics of multiply occupied religious places.

WHO DO YOU TRUST?

Antelope is a rural town in central Oregon, a three-hour drive southeast of Portland and an hour east of the Warm Springs Indian Reservation. Near here, on a 64,000-acre property, an intentional community called Rajneeshpuram thrived from 1981 to 1985. Precise numbers are unknown, but as many as 7,000 people lived at the commune. They were there because of one man, Bhagwan Shree Rajneesh, and his promises (Carter 1990; Goldman 1999; Lindholm 2003).

Rajneesh taught a form of anti-orthodox Indian mysticism that blended Eastern spiritual traditions with Western therapeutics. As a guru, Rajneesh promised his devotees (*sannyasin*) perfect enlightenment, transcendence of worldly concerns, unity, harmony, and ecstasy. Rajneesh left a successful ashram in India to develop the Oregon utopia, which he promoted as the place from which he and his devotees would rebuild society following the modern world's imminent collapse.

In Chapter 2 we discussed the ethics of ethnographic representation, and briefly met the Rajneeshee movement through the work of sociologist Marion Goldman. Through interviews with former female devotees, Goldman describes a group of well-educated, largely middle-class women who "chose to leave careers, friends, lovers, and sometimes families to follow a radical spiritual path" (2002: 146). By severing all connections with their everyday lives, devotees pursued one of the movement's central goals of self-loss. Within the commune, self-loss was practiced through participating in exhausting self-awareness groups, taking on new names, new birthdays, and eliminating all personal pronouns from speech (except for "He" in reference to Bhagwan). Dynamic meditation, Rajneesh's core ritual, also targeted self-loss. In this group ritual, always led by one of Bhagwan's disciples, devotees blindfolded themselves, danced to loud music, screamed, cried, laughed hysterically, and writhed on the ground as a way to replace their everyday consciousness with Bhagwan's promised enlightenment.

Increasingly, Rajneesh separated from all but a few of his closest disciples. Only selected devotees were permitted to see him. He claimed a heightened sensitivity to smell, bolstering his aura of purity, and devotees had to wash obsessively before requesting a visit. More often than not, they were still denied access. By his own description, Rajneesh's primary method was to confuse his followers. Through constantly changing the daily rules of Rajneeshpuram, and ordering mandates such as the temporary or permanent exchange of sexual partners, Rajneesh instilled a pervading mood of instability, uncertainty, and anxiety. Yet, to the very end when governmental authorities raided Rajneeshpuram, and still after when he rebuilt his Indian ashram under the new name of Osho, devotees maintained absolute trust in their guru.

THE PROBLEM OF AUTHORITY

In a startling way, the example of the Rajneeshee points us to a general problem in the anthropology of religion: the problem of authority. All religions—large and small, global and regional, marginal and mainstream—must provide adherents with a source of primary legitimacy. What do people invest with credibility, reverence, and awe? Or, taking this chapter's title, who do you trust? Religious authority can be moral, intellectual, existential, cosmological, institutional, bodily, social or, in many cases, all of the above. A productive question to ask of religious lives and worlds, then, is "How is authority understood, marshaled, asserted, managed, performed, internalized, challenged, and defended?"

More precisely, we might ask "Who (or what) do you trust?" For many new religious movements it is a question of who. We will say more about charismatic leadership below, but in some cases, like the Rajneeshee, there is no substitute for that central, compelling persona. There could only be one Bhagwan. But, religious authority can also be more dispersed: in objects, roles, institutions, and ritual constructs. Think about the category of "scripture" and an example like Islam. Muslims understand the Qur'an to be sacred because it is the written revelation of divine law, spoken directly from Allah to the prophet Muhammad. Or, think about the category of "clergy" and an example like the Roman Catholic papacy. In 2013, Jorge Mario Bergoglio became Pope Francis, the 266th Pope. The role itself is authoritative, not the individual. There were Popes before Francis and there will be Popes after. Rituals can also be authoritative. Consider an example like the practice of adult baptism in many Protestant traditions. There is no substitute for this act, which must be completed in a particular way. Centralized or dispersed, authority is crucial for understanding religious culture.

A core anthropological commitment is that the problem of religious authority is fundamentally social. This is true in two senses. First, authority does not just exist; it does not simply appear; it is not merely present. Authority must be established, produced and reproduced. Because authority is made, it is contingent. This is why we see challenges and disruptions to religious authority, and one reason that we see religions change over time. Second, religious authority is social because it is fundamentally relational. Authority forms and continues inter-subjectively. Be it between humans and God, humans and gods, humans and spirits, humans and ancestors, or humans and humans, authority exists between and among agents. Our ethnographic remit is to understand the dynamics of religious authority in lived cultural contexts: how it is made, reproduced, and contested. At times, this inquiry will center on how authority is performed and negotiated. Other times, it will center on how authority becomes inscribed into cultural conditions, institutional regimes, social fabrics, and individual lives. To help us on our way, consider three theoretical touchstones for exploring this problem of religious authority.

THREE TOUCHSTONES

We encountered the first theoretical touchstone in Chapter 1's discussion of how anthropologists have critiqued the category of "religion": Talal Asad's *Genealogies of Religion* (1993). If you recall, Asad critiqued the dominant approaches for studying religion, typified by Clifford Geertz's notion of "religion as a cultural system" (1966). He argued that when cultural products—symbols, beliefs, rituals—are analyzed apart from the social conditions and processes that produce them, we miss the opportunity to understand how those products are endowed with authority.

Asad sees this erasure as (wittingly or not) complicit in a theological agenda: "It is essential to keep clearly distinct that which theology tends to obscure: the occurrence of events (utterances, practices, dispositions) and the authorizing processes that gives those events meaning and embody that meaning in concrete institutions" (1993: 43). For example, it is one thing to study what a Muslim imam says about the Qur'an and quite another to study how Islamic textual ideologies are integrated into clerical training and mosque education. Asad helps us see that authority is an historical product of social processes; is present throughout the institutional infrastructure of religious life; and is equally relevant to the minutiae of everyday religious practice as it is to the most public, dramatic ritual ceremonies.

Max Weber, who we also met in Chapter 1, provides another major insight for addressing the problem of religious authority. Throughout his body of work Weber continually returned to the social hierarchies that define modern life. He distinguished between different kinds of authority, the two most prolific of which were "bureaucratic" and "charismatic" (1946 [1958]: 324–85). Neither is unique to religion. They are found in social arenas like politics and economics as well, but religious contexts bring them into particular relief.

Bureaucratic authority is oriented toward keeping the status quo, maintaining cultural conditions as they are, reproducing the legitimacy of an institutional order. The bureaucracy is "motivated by inertia" (Lindholm 2003: 358), resistant to large-scale change. The power of the bureaucrat is tethered to upholding the power of the institution. Bureaucratic leaders arrive in their position procedurally: appointed by another, elected by peers, or through succession. In the bureaucracy, the office itself is more powerful than any individual who occupies it at any given time. Weber saw this kind of authority dominating modern life's mainstream institutions.

Charismatic authority is the qualitative opposite of bureaucracy. It is tuned to change, disrupting the existing order, and institutional instability. Charismatic authority is oriented toward a specific persona. Weber defined charisma as "a certain quality of an individual personality by virtue of which he is considered extraordinary and treated as endowed with supernatural, superhuman or at least specifically exceptional powers or qualities" (1922 [1978]: 242). Unlike the inertia of bureaucracies, charisma is "motivated by emotion" (Lindholm 2003: 358). More precisely, it is an inter-subjective emotion; experienced between that extraordinary personality and those who he or she influences. The anthropologist Charles Lindholm describes it this way in his comparative study of charismatic authority: "Charisma is, above all, a relationship, a mutual mingling of the inner selves of leader and follower" (1990: 7).

The ideal types of bureaucracy and charisma are productive because they allow us to see religious leaders as diverse as Bhagwan Shree Rajneesh and the Roman Catholic Pope as emerging from the same problem of authority. Both rely on legitimacy, and the legitimacy to grant legitimacy. Both ask an audience to trust them, and to trust in the virtue of their decisions. But, they secure their authoritative status vis-à-vis different institutional orders. Weber also allows us to understand why movements like the Rajneeshee do not achieve longevity. Charismatic leaders die, disappear, and experience public failure. Movements organized around charismatic authority fail (slowly or abruptly) when no institutional structure develops to support and eventually replace the galvanizing figurehead who rallies people to a cause. Weber called the process of developing institutional longevity "the routinization of charisma."

This question of routinizing charisma has inspired many anthropologists, none more influentially than Anthony F.C. Wallace. In a 1956 article, "Revitalization Movements," Wallace asked how we could understand orchestrated cultural change. His opening premise is that models geared toward slow, gradual, undirected change cannot account for orchestrated change. Weber's charisma is key to his proposal. Wallace defined a revitalization movement as a "deliberate, organized, conscious effort by members of a society to construct a more satisfying culture" (1956: 265). He then outlined six phases of development for revitalization movements. (1) Following a period of deep disillusionment with society, an individual "reformulates" their vision of the world they live in and their own place in it. With rare exception, a single individual does this reformulation.

(2) That individual becomes a charismatic founder by teaching others about their new vision; "the dreamer ... becomes a prophet" (273). (3) Converts to the founder's vision are made and charismatic power is distributed beyond the single individual. (4) The newly established movement responds to resistance from mainstream (i.e., bureaucratic) society. This involves "adding to, emphasizing, playing down, and eliminating selected elements of the original visions" (274). (5) The movement witnesses the cultural transformation of its members, provoking "an enthusiastic embarkation on some organized program of group action" (275). (6) The movement witnesses itself becoming recognized, if not partially accepted, by mainstream society.

Weber and Wallace both emphasize the importance of anti-traditionalism in building charisma: generating a cultural critique of the existing order as a way to establish charismatic authority. Wallace also helps us remember that many outcomes can result from charismatic authorities: "some programs are literally suicidal; others represent well-conceived and successful projects of further social, political, or economic reform" (275). Yes, we have cases like The Peoples Temple, where Jim Jones orchestrated a mass suicide of 918 people in 1978 (an example which lends a chilling prescience to Wallace's writing in 1956). But, we also have examples like Wallace's key case study: the Handsome Lake revival (1799–1815), led by the Seneca prophet Handsome Lake, to unite the six Iroquois nations following widespread death and destruction at the hands of colonial settlers.

Our third theoretical touchstone comes from religious historian Bruce Lincoln's book, *Authority: Construction and Corrosion* (1994). Lincoln defines authority as a result or outcome of social life, not a thing in itself that exists outside of social life: "an effect, the capacity for producing that effect, and the commonly shared opinion that a given actor has the capacity for producing that effect" (10–11). This approach fits squarely within the anthropological commitment that authority must be actively made and remade in lived social contexts. Lincoln also extends Lindholm's inter-subjective description of charisma, identifying all forms of authority as fundamentally relational: "a posited, perceived, or institutionally ascribed asymmetry between speaker and audience" (4). He goes on to say that relations of authority are grounded in trust: "Authority depends on nothing so much as the trust of the audience, or the audience's strategic willingness to act as if it had such trust" (8).

Lincoln outlines a model in which authority can be both extremely powerful and highly contestable. Authority is exerted and it is challenged. It is obeyed and it is critiqued. It is internalized and it is rejected. It is persuasive and it is doubted. In this model, the power and contested nature of authority is performed through two broad sets of discourses: constructive and corrosive.

Constructive discourses are those that work to define, bolster, promote, support, buttress, and otherwise reproduce that "effect, the capacity for producing that effect, and the commonly shared opinion that a given actor has the capacity for producing that effect." (1994: 10) (In Weber's terms, both bureaucratic and charismatic authorities practice constructive strategies, but their strategies will mirror their respective institutional orders.)

Corrosive discourses work to challenge, erode, critique, damage, and otherwise impede or disrupt the maintenance of authority. Lincoln names "gossip, rumor, jokes, invective; curses, catcalls, nicknames, taunts; caricatures, graffiti, lampoon, satire; sarcasm, mockery, rude noises, obscene gestures" (78) as examples. (In Weber's terms, we might expect corrosive discourses to be more active in bureaucratic regimes, in which there is a defined institutional order. In a charismatic regime corrosive discourses would have to be far more subtle and covert, given the singular source of an authoritative individual.) Ultimately, Lincoln helps us remember that authority results from dynamic social processes and must be actively reproduced, negotiated, and contested.

So, with these theoretical touchstones in place, we are ready to explore some nuances of religious authority. The remainder of this chapter follows two lines of inquiry. In the first, "Locating authority," we examine where we observe authority being performed in the social life of religions. In the second, "Authority in dialogue," we examine how religious authority is entangled, often contentiously, with other sources of cultural authority. Before moving on, let's return to the Rajneeshee. After all, what happened after Oregon, 1985?!

Box 5.1 A revitalization movement?

Following the raid on Rajneeshpuram, Bhagwan Shree Rajneesh was deported from the United States. After being denied entry to numerous countries, he settled in his native India and, in 1987, began rebuilding his ashram in the city of Pune. In 1989 he changed his name to Osho and died in January 1990 ("left his body" as the *sannyasin* say). The Rajneeshee movement continues today as The Osho International Foundation (OIF).

Very clearly, Bhagwan Shree Rajneesh/Osho fits the bill of a charismatic leader and exemplifies Weber's charismatic authority. But, because the movement did not die with his death, is the OIF evidence that authority was successfully routinized?

To address this question, explore the OIF website: www. osho.com/visit. On your own, or with class colleagues, address these questions:

- How does the OIF actively produce authority? What are the constructive discourses at work? What is presented as an authoritative ritual or text? What are the sources of this authority?
- How well does the OIF match Wallace's model of successful revitalization?
- Finally, consider that this website makes use of mass media technology that was unavailable to Osho himself. What role does this virtual home play in the OIF's ongoing effort to maintain authority?

LOCATING AUTHORITY

Our organizing question for this section is: where do we find religious authority? While charismatic leaders, like Rajneesh, and bureaucratic leaders, like Pope Francis, are certainly compelling, they do not exhaust the locations of authority in religious life. There are other defined identities and roles to discuss, which we reference with the heading "Religious specialists." There are also other, less individual-centered, locations to discuss, which we reference with the heading "Ritual authority." Throughout, I hope this discussion reinforces the importance of understanding religious authority as a social product, one that is actively produced and contested, always embedded in lived relationships and contexts.

RELIGIOUS SPECIALISTS

The founders of new religious movements and the official heads of global religious institutions are but two kinds of religious personnel. The ethnographic record is replete with others: accounts of shamans, prophets, spirit mediums, priests, priestesses, oracles, sorcerers, diviners, folk healers, witch doctors, gurus, pastors, preachers, rabbis, imams, nuns, and monks. We can group these varying titles together under the rubric "religious specialist." This refers to a socially recognized role, in which authority is defined by the position of that role within a religious system and by how well the expectations of the system are satisfied by the specialist.

Anthropologists have relied on a helpful distinction between two broad categories: "Priest" and "Shaman." The heart of this distinction is that priests are full-time religious specialists who are subject to a hierarchal institutional order. Shamans are not part of a clear institutional order and are part-time specialists (i.e., they have other social, economic, or political roles that receive equal or more of their daily labor) (Klass 1995: 63–71). There are good reasons to be suspicious of this as an absolute divide. For example, while analytical categorization is helpful, it is not the end of our analysis. We have many questions still to ask about the everyday spiritual labors of priests and shamans after we identify what kind of religious specialist they are. Moreover, there is the misleading (and, ethnocentric) implication that these religious roles align with discretely different "complex" and "simple" societies. But, most anthropologists use the priest–shaman distinction as a kind of continuum for comparative purposes, not an absolute divide. It helps us understand why Methodist pastors are more like Jewish rabbis and Muslim imams than they are like Vodou priestesses or Azande sorcerers.

"Shaman" has proved to be a more ambiguous and debated comparative category. The term itself traces to the Evenk, an ethnolinguistic group of Eastern Siberia's Tungusic peoples (Bowie 2000: 191). A few features are regularly used to sketch out a minimum family resemblance for the category. First, there is an emphasis on methodology. Central to this is entering into a trance (or, altered state of consciousness) during a ritual event to commune with the spirits. This is often aided by techniques for inducing the altered state, for example: the ritual ingestion of mind altering substances, fasting, or sleep deprivation. Shamanic methodology also includes dedicated paraphernalia. This varies cross-culturally, but a few recurring examples include donning specialized clothing, playing ritual drums, and using specialized tools. There is also a defined period of training and apprenticeship that would-be shamans must complete, in which they learn how to conduct ritual events, and enter and control the altered state of consciousness (Stein and Stein 2010).

Shamanic authority is grounded in the ability to commune with the spirits, in having special access to or grasp on sacred truths. No anthropologist has ever reported about a shaman who only uses spiritual access for personal gain. Shamans, like charismatic prophets, are fundamentally social. Shamans use their spiritual access for healing (preventative and curative), divination (of secrets, of the future), mediation of troubles (fertility, protection), and invoking spiritual assistance (vengeance against an enemy, exorcism of evil). As these significant acts suggest, shamanic knowledge and practice is deeply powerful and, in many cases, considered dangerous to possess and use. Indeed, the ways of the shaman are often protected and kept secret from all non-shamans.

A bird's eye view of shamanic authority helps orient us, but we should zoom in on a case study for a close-up. Homayun Sidky began doing ethnographic work with Nepalese shamans (*jhakri*) in 1999. In a 2009 article (which includes exquisite fieldwork photography), Sidky tackles the question of how a shaman's altered state connects to a patient's healing. The spiritual remit of the *jhakri* "is to remedy crises and deflect anxieties and stresses that arise in the context of day-to-day interpersonal interactions which are frequently attributed to angry divinities or the malice of witches and evil spirits" (173). The *jhakri*'s key ritual performance is a 15–20-hour healing ceremony (*cinta*). During this ritual *jhakri* diagnose, heal, and demonstrate the superhuman powers afforded to them by their spiritual communion, such as "licking red-hot iron rods, eating burning wicks, stepping on hot coals, and consuming massive amounts of distilled liquor without ill effects" (175).

The article's central example is a *cinta* performed in 2007, located 20 miles from Katmandu (altogether, Sidky ethnographically documented 47 *cinta*). The patient was a 43-year-old local man suffering "from stomach and chest pains and tingling sensations throughout his body" (175). A team of shamans, headed by a senior *jhakri*, worked to divine the patient's diagnosis through dance and chant, and eventually fought a spiritual battle with Yamaraja, "'the God of Death,' who decides the fate of humans and exercises influence over planetary alignments that result in illness and death" (177). To contest Yamaraja, the senior *jhakri* channeled another spirit, Bhimsen Guru, as a "supernatural ally" (183). Possessed by Bhimsen Guru, the *jhakri* wielded two blades and physically attacked the invisible Yamaraja.

Ultimately, the *jhakri* emerged victorious, the patient was healed, and all present were purified by water and fire (including the ethnographer and his film crew). Sidky makes the important observation that this ritual healing is not simply about what a shaman does. Rather, it rests on a dynamic interaction among shaman, spiritual beings, patient, and the gathered crowd of patient's friends, family, and other locals. Moreover, the audience is not a set of passive onlookers; they actively discuss the proceedings as they unfold. This highlights the fundamentally relational nature of religious authority.

Shamanic authority is present in local village settings, like Sidky's Nepalese example, but it is also present in transnational encounters. Veronica Davidof writes about just such an encounter in a 2010 article, "Shamans and Shams." Davidof takes us to Ecuador's Amazon basin, and details how "traditional" and "new" shamans among the indigenous Kichwa struggle to define "real" shamanism amid ethno-, eco-, and jungle tourism encounters.

Kichwa shamans (variously called *yachajs* or *taitas* in Quechua, and *shamanos* or *curanderos* in Spanish), like their Nepalese counterparts, perform illness diagnosis, healing, divination, and "develop relationships with powerful spirits, who facilitate the shaman's passage into the spirit world" (Davidof 2010: 390). The *limpiada* is the Kichwa's central shamanic rite (akin to the *jhakri*'s *cinta*), and involves the ritual ingestion of *ayahuasca*, a hallucinogenic substance prepared from several naturally growing plants. One of Davidof's consultants, a retired shaman who is very critical of new shamans, claims that shamanic training should start as early as six years old, "before your sexuality develops," devote five years to *ayahuasca* mastery and two years to being an apprentice (396).

Ecuador's tourist boom, which began in the early 1980s, includes a diverse demographic of adventure tourists who desire an encounter with ethnic exotics. Such tourists are "in the market for radical alterity, which the indigenous [Ecuadorian] groups compete with each other to supply" (395). New shamans, whose training is ambiguous and not as extensive as that of traditionalists, will conduct *limpiadas* for tourist consumption, including the brewing and ingesting of *ayahuasca*. For an extra "off-the-books" (399) fee tourists can consume the plant too. Alterity-seeking travelers have no question that they have encountered "the real deal" (404):

> As the time-limited and experience-oriented tours privilege the performative and material sides of shamanism, rather than its esoteric spiritual traditions, the relationships between the lucrative enactment of shamanic rituals and one's identity as a shaman becomes complex, especially when the issue of legitimacy is at stake.
>
> (392)

Davidof avoids the morass of playing the "who's the authentic shaman" game for good reasons. For one, Kichwa debates about authenticity are not new to the global tourist era; they stretch back at least to the colonial encounter. Second, new shamans, while trained differently, are sincere practitioners of the *limpiada*; they cannot simply be dismissed as frauds. Instead, the local struggle to define shamanic authenticity illustrates how religious authority is up for grabs, contested in contexts of global tourism and changing indigenous economies.

Box 5.2 Global shaman networks

For the priest–shaman distinction, a key point is that priests are part of a hierarchical institutional order that judges legitimacy, while shamans are not. The formation of global shaman networks challenges this. These global networks are geared toward cultural revitalization, formation of virtual communities and, echoing the anxieties produced by Ecuador's shamanic authenticity debate, policing the boundaries of legitimate tradition. Explore three sites produced by and for Mongolian shamans:

- www.tengerism.org/
- www.tengerism.org/Buryat_Contents.html
- buryatmongol.org/

On your own, or with class colleagues, mine these sites for evidence of how shamanic authority is being defined. In particular, how is authority defined against "imposters" and other actors who are deemed as threats to shamanic authenticity? Before closing your discussion, be sure to consider how this example engages an organizing theme from this chapter's introduction. What do global shamanic networks illustrate about religious authority as a social process that must be produced, reproduced, and negotiated?

RITUAL AUTHORITY

In his landmark book, *Ritual and Religion in the Making of Humanity* (1999), Roy Rappaport wrote: "ritual, which also establishes, guards, and bridges boundaries between public systems and private processes, is *the* basic social act" (138; emphasis in original). This echoes a long-standing commitment in the anthropology of religion: ritual is the bread and butter of religion, an irreplaceable building block. In his book *Religion: An Anthropological View* (1966), Anthony F.C. Wallace suggests the same: "the goals of religion are to be achieved by performing rituals" (104). We have already seen several examples of ritual's importance in this chapter (e.g., Kichwa shaman's *limpiada*) and in previous chapters (e.g., Chapter 4's discussion of pilgrimage). In this section, we focus on ritual as the source and bearer of religious authority.

Throw a stone in anthropology's archives and you will hit a study of ritual. (Throw a bigger stone and you'll hit a definition). Every influential scholar of religion has written on the nature of ritual (see Bell (1997) for a review of ritual studies). Much like with "shaman," we can highlight a family of five common traits. (1) Ritual is marked as special vis-à-vis the ordinary flow of daily life. It is sometimes integrated into the flow of life (like prayer in many Christian traditions) and sometimes set apart as the peak of religious experience (like the Rajneeshee's dynamic meditation). (2) Ritual is ordered by a particular procedure and relies on exact execution to be authoritative. This quality holds up whether the ritual is brief or highly orchestrated. (3) Ritual is practiced in ways that are embodied and multi-sensory. This can require quite strenuous practice, such as the *jhakri*'s *cinta*. (4) Ritual is communicative. That is, it says something meaningful about something cultural to an audience. (5) Ritual is performative. That is, it does not merely reflect beliefs, values, commitments, or relationships; it can also generate them (recall Chapter 3's discussion of language pragmatics).

A lot of worthy attention in ritual studies is paid to the function of ritual. Emically, the purpose of ritual can be quite strategic: to heal an illness and influence the gods, as with the *jhakri*, or to move closer to perfect enlightenment, as with dynamic meditation. Etically, the purpose of ritual might be construed in the Durkheimian terms from Chapter 1. Collective rituals that sustain moral community are an integral dynamic of Durkheim's approach to religion (i.e., ritual promotes social cohesion even amid social instability). A ritual mechanism for this is what Durkheim called "collective efferves-cence," or the "physical experience of exaltation, intoxication, and self-loss" where "the visceral experience is prior to any message conveyed" (Lindholm 1990: 31, 35).

As you might guess, there are significant debates about the function-ality of ritual (see Bell 1997 for a review). But, our focus is elsewhere, on how rituals are the concrete social context for staging, legitimizing, and questioning religious authority. The ritual studies scholar Catherine Bell reminds us that ritual practices are not merely an instrument of religious power, they "are themselves the very production and negotiation of power relations" (1992: 196). To illustrate, we zoom in on an ethnographic example from northern Greece.

Every year, on May 21, a small group of Greek Orthodox Christians gather, play music, dance, light a large fire, spread the red-hot coals, and walk across them until the coals are extinguished. The ritual complex is called the Anastenaria and is performed by an ethnic minority known as Kostilides. The Kostilides settled in northern Greece as refugees after being twice displaced: once following the Balkan Wars of 1912–13 and again following Turkey's 1922 victory in the battle for Asia Minor. Ayia Eleni, a small village of less than a thousand people, is one of two places in Greece where the Anastenaria continues to thrive. This village is the site of Loring Danforth's stirring ethnography, *Firewalking and Religious Healing* (1989).

Only a small portion of Kostilides are Anastenarides, though the entire village supports and aids the ritual preparation. The majority of Anastenarides are women, which is significant because northern

Greece is quite patriarchal. This ritual provides a public context for women to display leadership and power, social assertions that are largely precluded in the ordinary course of everyday life. Anastenarides consider firewalking to be both dangerous and spiritually powerful, which means practitioners must experience a calling from God. This calling, which they term "suffering from the saint," is known by a diagnosis of symptoms: "unusual behavior involving fire … persistent dreams or visions involving Saint Constantine … periods of unconsciousness, paralysis, uncontrolled urination, or other involuntary or unacceptable behavior" (Danforth 1989: 81). To walk on fire the first time is to be healed from this suffering, and every time after is a celebration of healing, thanks, and devotion.

The ritual climax of the Anastenaria, May 21, is the festival of Saints Constantine and Helen in the Greek Orthodox liturgical calendar. Constantine, the first Roman Emperor to profess Christianity, and his mother Helen, are powerful saints throughout the Orthodox world. St. Constantine possesses the Anastenaria during the ritual, which is what protects them from being harmed by the fire. Their ritual act of faith, firewalking, "demonstrates whether people enter the fire with the power of the Saint (in which case they will not be burned) or whether they enter of their own volition (in which case they will be burned)" (127). While dramatic, the Anastenaria is "part of a more general attempt [among Orthodox Christians] to secure the beneficial effects of the supernatural power of God by establishing a personal relationship of mutual obligation with a particular saint" (71).

The firewalk is the peak of a lengthy ritual celebration. Prior to this culmination, adherents sing and dance throughout the day. The songs and dances are not unique to the ritual; they are traditional performances that connect the Kostilides to their ethnic past, a memory of life before displacement. Adherents approach the fire, dancing and singing, carrying sacred icons of Saints Constantine and Helen. The icons are painted wooden representations, often treasured family heirlooms. Throughout the year the icons are kept on home altars, prayed to and cared for. Carrying the icons insures possession and protection. Adherents walk and dance across the fire until the last ember has burned down and all is ash. Together, through the power of the Saints, Anastenarides ritually defeat the negative forces that threaten daily life and publicly declare their devotion. Annually, on May 21, they participate in a miracle.

While supremely uplifting for the Kostilides, individually and collectively, the Anastenaria is controversial. After settling in northern Greece in 1924, the ritual was practiced only in secret for fears of persecution by Orthodox Church officials. Those fears were realized in 1947, when the Anastenaria was performed in public for the first time. The Church of Greece accused them of being pagan worshippers, possessed not by Constantine but by satanic demons. Today, the impasse continues: Church officials denounce the ritual as sacrilege and adherents claim unique access to the power of the Saints.

The Anastenaria powerfully illustrates how religious ritual is the site of authority's construction and contestation. It is only through this specific event of firewalking, which culminates a ritual cycle and a ritual performance, that adherents can experience the possession and healing of St. Constantine. For women, it allows access to social power that they otherwise do not have. And, the ritual is a dividing point between a small group of Orthodox adherents and the Church's bureaucratic hierarchy.

Box 5.3 Pentecostal women and the power of testimony

Part of Danforth's account is the interplay of religion, gender, social power, and ritual authority. This dynamic reappears cross-culturally. A parallel example comes from Elaine Lawless' ethnography of Pentecostal women in the southern U.S. state of Indiana: *God's Peculiar People* (1988).

Lawless is trained as a folklorist and linguistic anthropologist, and focuses on the genres of speech that dominate Pentecostal worship: "The Pentecostal religious service is a stage for several different levels of performed verbal art" (59). One of Lawless' key arguments is that women use the spoken genre of "testimonies" to temporarily subvert their established cultural position as subordinate to male authority. In every worship service, time is allotted for congregants to stand and offer testimonies of faith. In these ritual moments, people are understood to be speaking not as their everyday selves, but under the inspiration of the Holy Spirit. Lawless found that women's testimonies frequently included explicit critiques of the congregation, including male pastors and other leaders. Such critiques never occurred outside the ritual context.

Along with the written ethnography, Lawless co-produced an ethnographic film. *Joy Unspeakable* (1981, 59 min.) is permanently archived for public use on a website dedicated to documenting American folklore: www.folkstreams.net/film,54. On your own, or with class colleagues, view this documentary with three questions in mind:

- How is the subordinate social position of Pentecostal women evident in speech, action, and social interaction?
- How do Pentecostal women use ritual contexts to generate authority for themselves?
- What else does the film illustrate about the deep entanglement between ritual and religious authority?

AUTHORITY IN DIALOGUE

In Chapter 1 we discussed Jose Casanova's secularization as differentiation thesis. This thesis resonates with the work of philosopher Charles Taylor in his book *A Secular Age* (2007). One of Taylor's central claims is that in Western modernity religious belief has become one option among many; it has lost the status of being a taken-for-granted imperative. Western moderns look to many sources for social, moral, historical, natural, and cosmological answers in addition to, or instead of, religion. The history of modernity that Taylor sketches is debatable (see Butler 2010), but his provocative argument highlights an extremely important social fact of contemporary life: religious authority is not the only game in town! Religious authority exists in a dynamic, and often contentious, relationship with other sources of cultural authority. This dynamic produces fascinating and complicated social arrangements that are best explored ethnographically. In this section, we profile examples of religious authority that exist in dialogue with other cultural institutions that make claims on public loyalty: the state and science.

RELIGION AND THE STATE

As political entities, states foster various kinds of relations with the phenomenon of religion and with particular religions. States can actively suppress religious affiliation and practice (recall Chapter 1's discussion of the Soviet Union). States can declare a specific religion as the official state religion, as Norway does with Lutheranism. States can function as theocracies, as Iran has done with Shia'a Islam since the 1979 Islamic Revolution. Or, as in nations like the United States, the state's official stance is one of non-interference in the free exercise of religion along with the prohibition of establishing a state religion. In any context, questions of legal structure and how individual laws impact religious expression are important. The power to establish laws and enforce punishment for violating laws is perhaps the most overt way in which state authority and religious authority clash with one another. Consider an example from native North America.

In 1978 the U.S. Congress passed the American Indian Religious Freedom Act. This federal law was geared toward protecting freedoms among traditional native religions. Native and non-native critics of the law argued that it was ineffectual because the vague legal language allowed too many conditions to be placed on the actual exercise of religious freedom. A clear example is the Native American Church (NAC) and its use of the peyote cactus. The NAC is an inter-tribal religious movement that began among Oklahoma tribes in the mid-1880s and declared its legal status as a church in 1918. Adherents look to the NAC for spiritual, mental, and physical healing, and the ritual ingestion of peyote is pivotal for effective healing. The NAC understands peyote to be "medicine," while the U.S. Drug Enforcement Agency classifies peyote as a dangerous and addictive Schedule I controlled substance because it contains the psychoactive ingredient mescaline. Federal- and state-level attempts to regulate and outlaw the ritual use of peyote stretch back to 1886.

This definitional clash was at the heart of the 1990 U.S. Supreme Court case, *Employment Division of Oregon v. Smith*. In 1984 Alfred Smith (Klamath tribe, Oregon) was working at a substance abuse treatment facility. His employer discovered his NAC affiliation and Smith was fired. He then filed for unemployment compensation on religious freedom grounds, but this was denied. The Oregon Court of Appeals reversed this decision and the Oregon Supreme Court upheld this reversal. However, the U.S. Supreme Court reversed the state court decision, denying compensation and challenging the religious legitimacy of ritual peyote use. *Oregon v. Smith* prompted the U.S. Congress to amend the American Indian Religious Freedom Act in 1994, strengthening the legal grounds specifically for ritual peyote use.

A Different Medicine (2013) is anthropologist Joseph Calabrese's ethnography of ritual peyote use among Navajo adherents in Arizona and New Mexico. Calabrese found the peyote ritual to be highly structured, organized, and controlled. Typically, an individual states a need for healing and a ceremony is arranged. A circular enclosure (most often, a tipi) with an east-facing opening is built. Four religious specialists lead the ritual: a Road Man (so named for the dominant NAC metaphor, "Life is a road") is the main organizer; a Drummer Man (responsible for drumming); a Fire Man (who tends the fire at the center of the circular enclosure); and a Cedar Man (who periodically places cedar incense in the fire). All ritual participants (patient, religious specialists, and family or friends of the patient) enter the circular enclosure at sundown, where they ingest peyote, pray, and sing until dawn the next morning (Calabrese 2013: 123).

Calabrese argues that "peyote is central to the Native American Church ... as a medicine, as a potent symbol, and as a spiritual entity" (101). As medicine (*azee* in Navajo), peyote is aimed at "higher order mental processes (such as self-awareness, problem solving, imagination, emotion, and suggestibility)" (26). The client requesting healing makes use of peyote's medicinal properties by seeking solutions to physical, mental, and spiritual problems: "beliefs are not simply transmitted from one member to another verbally; rather, it is believed that one must come upon one's beliefs independently through the sacramental experience of peyote consumption" (98). Calabrese stresses that peyote is not merely a means of healing. "Peyote is considered a benevolent guardian spirit or a messenger spirit allowing communication between humans and divinity" (104). "The most important therapeutic communications are those that come to the patient not from the [Road Man] but directly from God or the Peyote Spirit in the form of visions or other sacred experiences" (33). Beyond strict ritual use, Calabrese found through his ethnography that NAC adherents also use peyote to help socialize youth: "Peyote Meetings are held for children to support their schoolwork, and ingestion of the sacrament is thought to benefit children, as well as adults" (152).

Ritual peyote use among NAC adherents is one example of what happens when the authority of the state clashes with religious authority. Is peyote sacramental medicine or a dangerous drug? Who do you trust to decide this: the U.S. government or the NAC? This is an instructive example because it shows how the clash is worked out within the context of a general religion–state culture (the constitutional provision regarding free exercise of religion). Moreover, claims of religious freedom are not uncontested by the state, whence the fluidity between 1886, 1978, 1990, 1994, and beyond. After all, how far outside the boundaries of ritual will U.S. courts protect the NAC right to peyote use? And, who will the U.S. courts protect as a legitimate NAC adherent?

Box 5.4 Celestial marriage

On April 3, 2008, governmental authorities raided a 1,700-acre ranch outside Eldorado, Texas (a three-hour drive west from the capital city of Austin). The ranch belonged to a Fundamentalist Church of Jesus Christ of Latter-Day Saints (FLDS) community who practice polygyny; or, in emic terms, "celestial marriage." State police acted on reports of child abuse and sexual assault, ultimately placing over 400 children in foster care. At the time, it was the largest governmental seizure of children in U.S. history. It was not, however, the first mass governmental targeting of Mormon polygynists. Similar raids occurred in the Utah–Arizona border town of Short Creek in 1953 and 1944. Here, the clash of religious and state authority revolves around questions of gender, sexuality, and kinship (Jacobson and Burton 2011).

Mormon polygyny dates near to the movement's origins. Joseph Smith, the founding charismatic prophet, received the revelations that were eventually published as *The Book of Mormon* in the 1820s. In 1843, Smith reported a revelation advocating celestial marriage as a divine calling. As Latter-Day Saint (LDS) communities proliferated in the American West, the religion–state clash escalated, culminating in The Edmunds Act of 1882 declaring plural marriage a felony. Bigamy of any kind remains illegal in every U.S. state. In 1890, partly as an attempt to gain statehood for Utah, the LDS Church officially disavowed plural marriage. LDS members who continued to practice celestial marriage were forced to leave the Church beginning around 1905, and the modern fundamentalist Mormon movement was organized in the late 1920s at Short Creek. Today, there are at least 20,000 Mormon polygynists (a very small percentage of the nearly 6.5 million LDS members in the United States), divided among four major groups, living throughout the Intermountain West of the United States, Canada, and Mexico (Jacobson and Burton 2011).

For fundamentalist Mormons, celestial marriage is about eternal salvation far more than sexual desire or romantic love (Miles 2011). "The Principle," as the divine calling to celestial marriage is often called, is grounded in several theological commitments. Most important, it is about expanding the kingdom of saints: a system of multiple wives can produce and care for children exponentially faster than monogamy. And while some believe that polygyny advances the glory of pious men, celestial marriage emerges from a literalist reading of Isaiah 4:1 concerning the overabundance of godly women in the messianic age: "In that day seven women will take hold of one man and say, 'We will eat our own food and provide our own clothes; only let us be called by your name. Take away our disgrace!'" (New International Version). Mormon fundamentalists also tie polygyny to their cultural critique of mainstream life: "[It] is said to remove the evils of modern society, which include single motherhood, single career women, and widespread divorce … it would wipe out prostitution, infidelity, homosexuality, spinsterhood, childlessness, and other types of sexual sin" (Bennion 2011a: 109–10). Based on 15 years of ethnographic work in multiple fundamentalist Mormon communities, anthropologist Janet Bennion argues that celestial marriage is not inherently abusive, but rather entails distinct benefits and forms of female empowerment, including creative strategies for dispersing household responsibilities (Bennion 2011b: 170–4).

Mormon polygyny raises provocative questions about the clashing of religious and state authority. What counts as an abuse of religious freedom in the United States? Who has the power to define what legitimate marriage is? How do we arrive at decisions about a consensual marriage age? What is the best structure for a family household, and who do we trust to define this? Unlike the example of the Native American Church, Mormon polygyny exists at an impasse. These communities live in open violation of federal and state law. In theory, further governmental seizures of children could happen on any given day.

On your own, or with class colleagues, explore some primary source material about Mormon polygyny from different mass media genres:

- As the major newspaper of Utah, *The Salt Lake Tribune* devotes an exclusive archive to Mormon polygamy (www. sltrib.com/cat/polygamy). You can also find opinion pieces written by Mormon fundamentalists. For example, there is this one from Maggie Jessop, the daughter of an influential polygynous prophet, in response to the Texas raids: "I am an FLDS woman and I am entitled to the same rights as you" (www.sltrib.com/opinion/ci_9211573). How do advocates like Maggie Jessop support religious authority and challenge state authority?

- Following the success of HBO's *Big Love* (2006–11), a drama series that portrays an independent polgynyist family living in Salt Lake City, several television networks have created series in the 'Reality TV' genre: for example, National Geographic Channel's *Polygamy USA* (http:// channel.nationalgeographic.com/channel/polygamy-usa/) and TLC's *Sister Wives* (www.tlc.com/tv-shows/sister-wives). How do these representations address the clashing of religious and state authority?

- There are numerous memoirs written from a variety of standpoints, including former fundamentalist wives (e.g., Carolyn Jessop's *Escape*), excommunicated fundamentalist men (e.g., Brent Jeffs' *Lost Boy*), and independent polygynists advocating for celestial marriage (e.g., Joe, Alina, Vicki, and Valerie Darger's *Love Times Three*). Read a sample from each. How do they represent the everyday life of celestial marriage? How do their representations articulate the entanglement of religious authority and state authority?

RELIGION AND SCIENCE

The relationship between religion and science has a long history in the anthropology of religion. In *The Golden Bough* (1890) James Frazer famously used magic, religion, and science as mileposts to mark the progressive cultural evolution from so-called "primitive" to modern societies. More ethnographically, Bronislaw Malinowski argued in *Magic, Science and Religion and Other Essays* (1948) that "primitive" peoples used magic in very rational, empirical, and effective ways to organize their everyday life. Robin Horton's essay on "African Traditional Thought and Western Science" (1967) follows up on Malinowski's critique of magic and religion as anti- or non-rational systems. Horton insists on a fundamental divide between traditional religions and modern science, the former characterized by an unawareness of competing explanations and an anxiety around protecting a sacred worldview. Evolutionary anthropologists continue to compare religion and science as intellectualist frameworks (e.g., Pascal Boyer's *Religion Explained* (2001) and Scott Atran's *In Gods We Trust* (2002)). And, Bruno Latour (2005) argues for an anthropological recalibration: that religion is concerned with the here and now, the visible, the concrete, whereas science is about the transcendent, invisible world. Instead of seeing religion and science as competing or overlapping, Latour argues that "there is no point of contact between the two, no more, let's say than nightingales and frogs have to enter into any sort of direct ecological competition" (35).

Dwelling on where to mark the epistemological and ontological boundaries between religion and science is not our only option. We can also study how religion and science are culturally entangled, how they interact in lived social contexts. Given the substantial economic and political power of science in modernity, a primary ethnographic question is how scientific authority impacts religious authority. Once again, who do you trust?

The anthropology of Protestant creationism is an exemplary case of how religion and science are framed as competing authorities. The term "creationism" covers a wide range of theological and cultural stances (Scott 2004), but we use it in this section as shorthand for a particular variant of Christian fundamentalism that is organized by five commitments. (1) The Christian Bible is believed to be the perfect "Word of God," ultimately authoritative over any other source on all matters (moral, cosmological, historical, etc.). (2) Human beings are a special creation "made in God's image," which forecloses any possibility that humans evolved from any kind of primate ancestor. (3) A literal reading of the Bible's first book, Genesis, reveals that God created the universe—including Earth, human beings, and the basic skeleton of Earth's biodiversity—in its current form roughly 6,000 years ago. This means that humans must have co-existed with every animal for which there is fossil evidence, including dinosaurs. (4) A universal flood killing all but eight people, detailed in Genesis 6–9, was a real historical event with geological and biological implications. Geologically, the Deluge of Noah is the basis for creationist "flood geology," which is said to explain geologic formations (e.g., Arizona's Grand Canyon) and archeological finds (e.g., fossil distribution). Biologically, today's global population, in all its ethnic and linguistic diversity, can be traced to Noah's three sons: Shem, Ham, and Japheth. (5) Biblical authority is under threat in modernity. The primary antagonist is evolutionary science, which creationists believe is inherently corrupting and the root cause of many (if not most!) social and moral problems.

While creationism is a global phenomenon (Coleman and Carlin 2004), the modern movement is North-American-born and this discussion has in mind its cultural shape in the United States. The intellectual genealogy of creationism traces to Ellen White, the founding prophetess of the Seventh-day Adventist denomination. In 1864 White published her divine revelations of a six-day creation and Noah's flood. One of White's disciples, George McCready Price, popularized this literal Genesis history in several books beginning in 1902. In the 1920s influential evangelicals, such as the circuit preacher Billy Sunday, linked evolutionary science with moral plagues like Nazi eugenics. In the summer of 1925 the creationist–evolutionary science conflict became international news when the famous Scopes Trial ruled that a high school biology teacher was guilty of teaching evolution in a Tennessee public school. (At the time, the trial set a record for producing 2,000,000 telegraph words!)

While McCready's books and the Scopes Trial galvanized creationists, the movement did not crystallize until the 1960s. It began with the publication of *The Genesis Flood* by two fundamentalist writers, followed by a series of landmark U.S. Supreme Court cases (outlawing prayer in public schools, barring compulsory Bible reading in public school classrooms, and authorizing the teaching of evolutionary science in public schools). The success of the creationist movement was evident in the 1980s, as numerous states legislatures introduced bills that requested public school science teachers to devote "equal time" to evolutionary science and creationism. In the 1990s numerous state school boards voted to add notes and disclaimers to biology textbooks, informing students that there is a "scientific controversy" about the origins of life on Earth (see Numbers (1992) for an in-depth history of modern creationism).

In his ethnography, *God's Own Scientists* (1994), anthropologist Christopher Toumey analyzes how a select group of creationists manage the tension between religious and scientific authority. Toumey interviewed 51 creationists working in science professions, primarily laboratory and medical settings. An intriguing finding was that creationists in these contexts experience little turmoil between their religious convictions and the daily operations of conducting scientific experiments. Toumey argues that because their work is largely removed from mainstream science's theoretical debates and questions of natural history, creationists who are not on the frontlines of national debate can exempt themselves from the frame of religion–science conflict.

The anthropologist Ella Butler examines a different group of creationists in a 2010 article. In "God Is in the Data," she analyzes the $30 million Creation Museum that opened in northern Kentucky in 2007, and interviews some of the individuals who designed the museum's content. There are at least two dozen such "creation museums" throughout the United States, but the Kentucky museum is by far the most ambitious. The museum was built by "Answers in Genesis," America's largest creationist ministry founded in 1994. Central to the work of the ministry and the museum is to demonstrate how "creation science" and evolutionary science differ in their sources of authority ("God's Word v. human reason"), and how "biblically-based science" supports creationists' five commitments. Butler illustrates how the Creation Museum uses selected language, symbols, and technologies of mainstream science to bolster biblical authority, all the while communicating within the authoritative frame of a "museum." In historical perspective, Answers in Genesis continues the work of earlier evangelists who designed mass media cultural productions to integrate the dual authorities of fundamentalism and science, such as the Moody Institute of Science in 1945 (Gilbert 1997).

Box 5.5 Holy healthy

To continue working with the entanglement of religious and scientific authorities, we can return to an ethnographic example from Chapter 3: the African Hebrew Israelites of Jerusalem (AHIJ). This movement—which began in Chicago in the 1960s and is now centered in Dimona, Israel—claims to be one of the Lost Tribes of the biblical Hebrews and thus God's chosen people. In Chapter 3 we discussed how the AHIJ use the body as a site of religious discipline, namely through their unique invention of vegan soul food. The AHIJ dietary regimen, and in turn their project of cultivating holiness, involves an appeal to scientific authority (Jackson 2013).

In 2009, the African Hebrew Development Agency (a development branch of the Israelite movement) partnered with the Ghanaian Ministry of Health to teach a program of "regenerative wellness" to Ghanaian communities. From Chicago to Dimona to Ghana, the movement's entry into transnational development work is grounded equally in scripture and claims of scientific legitimacy. On your own, or with class colleagues, listen to the AHIJ explain their project (http://africanhebrewisraelitesofjerusalem.com/?page_id=41). These three videos (c.20 minutes total) are promotional material produced by the AHIJ in support of their Ghanaian development efforts. After listening, consider how the AHIJ integrates religious authority with scientific authority. To go further, you can compare how the AHIJ engagement with science compares with Answers in Genesis' Creation Museum (http://creationmuseum.org/).

CODA

The two examples in this section, the state and science, reveal how religious authority is maintained in dynamic relationship with other sources of authority. This is a pivotal observation because it recognizes that religion does not exist on an island unto itself, detached from the rest of social life. Rather, it is always entangled with other powerful institutions. It is also not incidental that both examples have deep associations with modernity. This returns us to Taylor's argument mentioned at the outset: religious belief is but one option among many for moderns. Put differently: the religious voice is not the only voice that commands the attention of modern people. Ethnographically, our remit is to head for the center of these entanglements, where religious authority and other authorities vie for public loyalty.

Of course, the examples profiled here only scratch the surface of possibilities. Religions are entangled with many other modern institutions. To continue further, consider the modern exemplar of global capitalism. You can begin with two ethnographic case studies, one of Indonesian Islam and the other of charismatic Christianity in Mexico. Daromir Rudnyckyj's *Spiritual Economies* (2010) and Peter Cahn's *Direct Sales and Direct Faith in Latin America* (2011) both explore how religious and capitalist logics become fused in powerful institutions and individual lives. (Note: both have representative articles you can start with—Rudnyckyj 2009 and Cahn 2008).

CHAPTER SUMMARY

In this chapter, we explored the problem of religious authority. In the course of religious lives and worlds, who (and what) do people trust? Charismatic movements, deeply institutionalized religions, scriptures, rituals, divine speech, shamanic healing, marriages, museums, and health programs: all express this same problem. We have seen throughout that religious authority is actively reproduced, negotiated, and contested amid dynamic social processes.

Our discussion followed two lines of inquiry: the locations of religious authority, and the ways in which religious authority is maintained in dialogue with other sources of cultural authority. In doing so, we covered a range of ethnographic examples: traditional shamans in Nepal and competing definitions of authentic shamanism in Ecuador ("Religious specialists"); Greek Orthodox firewalkers and Pentecostal women in Indiana ("Ritual authority"); the Native American Church and celestial marriage among fundamentalist Mormons ("Religion and the state"); young earth creationists and the African Hebrew Israelites of Jerusalem ("Religion and science").

Ultimately, I hope this chapter excites your interest in the anthropology of religion in two ways. First, the examples and theoretical insights gathered here demonstrate that religious authority is, in fact, a fundamental empirical problem for the ethnographic study of religion. At first glance, we may find no conceptual link between firewalking and celestial marriage. But, positing authority as an underlying problem that religious adherents are resolving allows us to connect them. Second, what other cultural formations do you see emerging from the problem of religious authority? How else are religious specialists invested with trust, accountability, and awe? What rituals allow adherents to experience, internalize, or challenge religious authority? And, what other sources of cultural authority must religions in the modern world engage? The more attuned we are to these questions, the more we practice a robust, inspiring, and productive anthropology of religion.

SUGGESTIONS FOR FURTHER READING

Along with the works cited in this chapter, consider these books and essays as productive next places to go. To follow up on "The problem of authority," *The Anthropology of Religious Charisma: Ecstasies and Institutions* (Palgrave Macmillan, 2013) gathers ten anthropological essays that elaborate on charismatic power. For an ethnographic example, there is Barry Lyons' *Remembering the Hacienda: Religion, Authority, and Social Change in Highland Ecuador* (University of Texas Press, 2006). To continue with "Locating authority," an ethnography about shamans at the center of transnational politics is Marjorie Balzer's *Shamans, Spirituality, and Cultural Revitalization: Explorations in Siberia and Beyond* (Palgrave Macmillan, 2011). For an innovative study of ritual, there is Matt Tomlinson's *Ritual Textuality: Pattern and Motion in Performance* (Oxford University Press, 2014). To further explore "Authority in dialogue," Peter van der Veer's *The Modern Spirit of Asia: the Spiritual and the Secular in China and India* (Princeton University Press, 2014) examines contested relationships between religions and states. For a historical ethnography of religion in dialogue with science, there is Pamela Klassen's *Spirits of Protestantism: Medicine, Healing, and Liberal Christianity* (University of California Press, 2011).

GOING GLOBAL

Every October since 2002, a nearly 3,000-mile relay run begins at the Basilica of Guadalupe in Mexico City. Built in 1976 near Tepeyac Hill, the Basilica is Mexico's most popular religious site and one of the world's most visited Catholic pilgrimage sites. For believers, Tepeyac is the site where the Virgin Mary appeared to a Mexican peasant named Juan Diego in December 1531. Pope Benedict XIV formally recognized Juan Diego's apparition as authentic in 1754. The Virgin of Guadalupe is now both a Mexican national symbol and an icon of global Catholicism.

The relay run ends on December 12, Our Lady of Guadalupe Feast Day, at St. Patrick's Cathedral in Manhattan. Runners carry a lit torch, wear shirts that read *Mensajeros por un pueblo divide por la frontera* (Messengers for a people divided by the border) and hold images of the Virgin as they move northeast into Texas, the Louisiana swamps, Mississippi, Alabama, Georgia, South Carolina, North Carolina's piedmont region, Virginia, Washington D.C., Maryland, Delaware, Pennsylvania, New Jersey, and finally into New York. Along the way, supporters cheer for the runners, kissing or touching either the torch or the Marian images. In Manhattan, thousands of supporters wait with Marian statues, paintings, tattoos, emblems, and jewelry to greet the final runner. *La Antorcha Guadalupana* (The Guadalupan Torch Run) connects Catholic religious history and performance with North American political debates about immigration rights and citizenship, emotional bonds among friends and kin, the human costs of migrant labor, and other transnational flows between Mexico and the United States (Galvez 2009).

This ritual event reminds us of an important fact: religion has played a central role in making global networks and crossing borders for a long time. Think of Christian and Islamic missionaries, who have connected faraway places by crossing national, ethnic, and linguistic borders since the 1st and 7th centuries, respectively. This deep history frames our final research problem: what relationships exist between global formations and religious worlds? In this chapter we will explore two expressions of this problem: religious identity among diasporic groups and transnational religious cultures. To start, we establish some theoretical and methodological bearings.

RELIGIOUS GLOBALIZATION

Our discussion begins by unpacking the term most pivotal for this chapter's analysis: "globalization." Studies of globalization have been a dominant concern for cultural anthropologists since the early 1980s. The anthropological fascination with all things global and transnational springs from many sources. Some sources reflect perennial anthropological questions, like what happens when different cultures come into contact. Other sources reflect patterns and questions that emerge from our contemporary world, like the intertwined fates of indigenous groups, humanitarian activists, nation-states, and multinational corporations. In any case, globalization has become one of those unavoidable phenomena that all anthropologists consider as part of their research.

So, what is globalization? We compare some definitions below (akin to our work in Chapter 1 with "religion"), but most discussions of the term begin with a wise reminder: what we now call "globalization" is not a new phenomenon. There are substantial historical precedents. We might highlight the Spice Trade and Silk Road that connected China to the Mediterranean as early as 3000 BCE. Several centuries of colonialism began in the 1500s, in which Western European nations like Portugal, Spain, Britain, the Netherlands, and

France exerted power (often brutally) throughout Asia, Africa, and the Americas. And, colonial contact bred other global formations, such as missionization, the transatlantic slave trade and the world's first multinational corporation, the Dutch East India Company (1602–1798) (Wolf 1982).

When contemporary anthropologists talk about "globalization," we recognize these deep historical roots, but refer more particularly to the post-World–War-II era and, even more recently, a political–economic shift that has spread throughout the world from the early 1970s onward. This shift is usually termed "neoliberalism," which refers to a form of global capitalism that favors free market exchange, decreased trade regulations, and increased privatization of industry and services. But, globalization should not be reduced to a political–economic ideology. There are many forms of cultural globalization, including examples like the transnational spread of foodways, art, music, dance, cinema, fashion, sport, entertainment, and, of course, religion. This is why some scholars prefer the term "transnationalism," because it highlights such constant back-and-forth flows without the neoliberal connotation of "globalization" (Lewellen 2002).

So, how has globalization been defined by social scientists as a phenomenon and a process to be studied ethnographically? Table 6.1 presents seven representative examples.

Consider five observations about these seven definitions. (1) Words like "intensification," "increasing," and "accelerated" indicate a focus on processes of accumulating force. There is a sense that globalization has inertia, which is experienced in the everyday lives of people. (2) Several definitions foreground the existence of "flows" that cross different kinds of boundaries. Flow connotes constant movement and circulation, which is central to one of the most widely cited frameworks for studying globalization. The transnational-scapes model outlined by Arjun Appadurai (1996) identifies a series of intersecting flows that shape contemporary life: people (ethnoscapes), technology (technoscapes), finance (financescapes), media (mediascapes), and ideas (ideoscapes). (3) Words like "compression" and "reorganization" suggest that there have been transformations in the way modern people relate to time and space. The world can feel smaller, social change can seem to happen at a faster pace, and attachments to place can experience drastic rupture. (Here, you might revisit Chapter 4

Table 6.1 Social science definitions of "globalization"

Definition	Source
The intensification of worldwide social relations which link distant localities in such a way that local happenings are shaped by events occurring many miles away and vice versa.	Giddens (1990: 63)
The compression of the world and intensification of consciousness of the world as a whole.	Robertson (1992: 8)
The creation of new economic, financial, political, cultural, and personal relationships through which societies and nations come into closer and novel types of contact with one another.	Waters (2001: 80)
The increasing flow of trade, finance, culture, ideas, and people brought about by the sophisticated technology of communications and travel and by the worldwide spread of neoliberal capitalism and the local and regional adaptations to and resistance against these flows.	Lewellen (2002: 7)
An intensification of global connectedness [and] a basic reorganization of time and space.	Inda and Rosaldo (2002: 5)
Accelerated flows or intensified connections—across national and other boundaries—of commodities, people, symbols, technology, images, information, and capital, as well as disconnections, exclusions, marginalizations, and dispositions.	Edelman and Haugerud (2005: 2)
Condition by which people, commodities, and ideas literally cross—transgress—national boundaries and are not identified with a single place of origin.	Watson (2006: 11)

and consider the close analytical links between these two chapters.) (4) There is a stress on the "relations" or "connectedness" of the local and the non-local. This is a social experience in that local groups and non-local groups encounter and develop ties with one another. It is also psychological and affective; there is an altered "consciousness" about what it means to live as part of this locally/non-locally connected world. And (5), most of these seven definitions highlight agency and power. Anthropologists understand globalization to be defined by human strategies of adaptation and resistance, as well as exclusion, marginalization, and other experiences of inequity.

ETHNOSCAPES, MEET SACROSCAPES

Globalization is the 21st century sea we swim in, both as scholars and as people in the world. How can we conceptualize the relationships that exist between global dynamics and religious worlds? One model comes from Thomas Tweed (2006), a historian and ethnographer of American religions. Tweed elaborates on Appadurai's notion of -scapes and suggests that we think in terms of "sacroscapes." He writes that religions "move across time and space. They are not static. And they have effects. They leave traces. They leave trails" (62). To think in terms of sacroscapes means that we think in terms of "the multiple ways that religious flows have left traces, transforming people and places, the social arena and the natural terrain" (ibid.). For Tweed, this approach emerged from his fieldwork with Cuban Catholics who migrated to Miami in the wake of the 1950s Cuban Revolution. Understanding Cuban American Catholicism meant focusing on sacroscape themes: transnational flows of faith as well as people, belief as well as money, ritual as well as citizenship. Elizabeth McAlister (2005), an ethnographer of Haitian religions, has proposed a similar approach. She argues that there is an important relationship between religion and the varieties of ethnoscapes in our contemporary world: labor migration, forced displacement, and exile. Tweed and McAlister both capitalize on the anthropological concept of holism by stressing the important ties between religion and other social processes (namely, economic and political changes).

As people traverse borders, what makes religion something good to travel with? The anthropologist Paul Johnson (2012) highlights two reasons. First, migrants can "carry religion with them more easily" (95) than other aspects of self and community that are more difficult to manage and transport. Second, religion "acquires particular weight as an anchor of collective identity and distinction" (ibid.) amid the dislocating nature of transnational mobility. Migration tends to draw out religion's ability to facilitate social and affective belonging. Some of the examples we explore below highlight these good-for-traveling qualities of religion, but transnational mobility can also be disruptive to religious identity. In other examples below, the flows that characterize sacroscapes confront adherents with questions of authenticity. This is especially true when religion is definitively associated with a homeland place. "Is doing religion *here* the same as doing it *there*?" As you consider the ethnographic examples presented throughout this chapter, ask when Johnson's two reasons are evident, if any other reasons become visible, and how groups go about resolving questions of authenticity.

The anthropologist Thomas Csordas (2009) also proposed a useful framework for making sense of religious globalization. For Csordas, religions successfully globalize when they cultivate two qualities: "portable practice" and "transposable message." Portability refers to "rites that can be easily learned, require relatively little esoteric knowledge or paraphernalia, are not held as proprietary or necessarily linked to a specific cultural context" (4). In other words, the easier it is to perform the rituals that are important to religious life, the more likely that religion will thrive in multiple places. On the other hand, transposability is about "the basis of appeal contained in religious tenets, premises, and promises [establishing a] footing across diverse linguistic and cultural settings" (5). In other words, how durable are core religious assumptions as they get translated into new contexts? (Here, Csordas' "basis of appeal" expresses the problem of religious authority discussed in Chapter 5.) As you consider the ethnographic examples below, ask how these qualities of portability and transposability are at work.

Box 6.1 The Guadalupan Torch Run as sacroscape

We opened this chapter with an example: the Virgin of Guadalupe at the center of a transnational ritual. On your own, or with class colleagues, use this example to reflect on the key terms, themes, and questions from this introductory section.

- In our review of definitions we observed that globalization is a process that: has inertia, is marked by flows, compresses time and space, elevates connectedness, and reveals dynamics of agency and power. How do these apply for our understanding of The Guadalupan Torch Run?
- With the notion of sacroscapes, Tweed emphasizes how religious flows transform individuals, communities, social contexts, and places. How is this true for The Guadalupan Torch Run?

- Following Johnson (2012), religion has adaptive capacities amid global formations that can often be disruptive and challenging. For The Guadalupan Torch Run, why is religion a good resource for performing transnational activism?
- Consider another useful concept. In a 2006 article, anthropologists compared ethnographic data from Nigerian migrants in two cities: Halle, Germany and Manchester, New Hampshire (Glick-Schiller *et al.* 2006). They argue that all migrants face the problem of "incorporation": building social networks in new places that will produce senses of affiliation, belonging, and exchangeable forms of social capital. In this example, Nigerian migrants relied on local Protestant congregations to incorporate, which contrasts with the expectation that migrants rely primarily on ethnic-based networks. How might The Guadalupan Torch Run help Mexican migrants' incorporation in the United States?

RELIGION IN DIASPORA

In this section we examine one expression of religious globalization: practicing religion in diaspora. Four features define diasporic groups: dispersion from an original homeland, collective memory of the homeland, maintenance of ties with the homeland, and an ongoing experience of difference with the new place of belonging (Johnson 2007). Fundamentally, then, diasporas are about a relationship with multiple places. The remembered and continued connections with a homeland and the tensions of adjusting to a new home foster "a double consciousness" about place that is "actively conjured" (Johnson 2007: 31). What role can religion play in this double consciousness?

In his comparative ethnography of Garifuna religion at home (in coastal Honduras) and in diaspora (in New York City), Paul Johnson (2007) argues that diasporic religion is a specific kind of religious culture. Tweed (1997), in his study of Miami's Cuban Catholics, also argues that diasporic religion is distinctive because it is "translocative" and "transtemporal." What he means by this is that religious identity and practice forge connections between old and new homes as well as remembered pasts and imagined futures. (Again, consider how the lessons we discussed in Chapter 4 aid our work in this chapter.) Diasporic religions are also distinctive because of how they confront the problem of continuity across generations. Children of migrants can be less likely to follow their parents' tradition; sometimes because there are new religious options available and other times because migrant children experience the marginalization of being a marked Other in society. But, this sense of Otherness can go both ways, provoking some to want distance from the religion of their parents and others to place renewed value on traditional religious belonging. For example, in the Jewish diaspora the "dispersion was not merely a loss but also a great source of vitality" (Johnson 2012: 42). All this helps articulate a question that you can consider throughout this section: In what ways is diasporic religion a distinctive form of religious identity and practice?

HINDUISM IN DIASPORA

Hinduism is an excellent example for thinking about diasporic religion because a particular place, India, is integral for this religious tradition. The main Hindu scriptures—the *Vedas* and *Upanishads*—were composed in the ancestral homeland of the Indus Valley between 1500 and 500 BCE. The Indian subcontinent is home to most Hindu pilgrimage sites (temples and holy cities). And, modern-day India is home to approximately 886 million Hindus, by far the largest concentration in any nation. Distinctions like "modern-day India" are important because there are competing ideas among Hindus as to where exactly the spiritual homeland is located. Is it the entire Indus Valley? Is it colonial British India (1858–1947), which includes Pakistan, Bangladesh, and Sri Lanka? Or, is it the modern nation-state of post-colonial India?

Vineeta Sinha (2011), in an ethnography of Hindus living in Singapore and Malaysia, affirms the importance of India for this diasporic religion: "Grounding 'Hinduism' in India's mythological, cultural, and physical landscape means that India as the 'home of Hinduism,' has a looming presence in Hindu diasporic consciousness, even if the 'myth of eventual return' is absent" (25). As of 2011, there were approximately 69 million Hindus living outside India (as few as 3,100 in Sweden and as many as 500,000 in South Africa). The global dispersion of Hindus owes to two separate migration periods, and in the remainder of this section we consider one ethnographic example from each migration. The first dates to the 1830s, when lower-caste Hindus were transported to far-flung locales like the Caribbean islands to work as indentured servants on agricultural plantations. The second wave of Hindu migration occurred after India's independence from Britain. Unlike the previous wave of farm laborers, post-1947 migrants are typically well-educated, speak English as a first language, and are well schooled in the aesthetics and values of global cosmopolitanism.

FIRST MIGRATION: MAURITIUS

Our first example comes from Mauritius, an island in the Indian Ocean, about 500 miles east of Madagascar. There, linguistic anthropologist Patrick Eisenlohr did fieldwork with a local population of Indian Hindus who descend from indentured laborers brought to work the island's sugar plantations by British colonizers beginning in 1834.

In his ethnography, *Little India* (2006), Eisenlohr describes Mauritius as a multi-ethnic nation dominated by Indians. Almost 70 percent of the country's 1.2 million people are of South Asian origin, 52 percent of whom are Hindu and the rest Muslim. The remaining 30 percent of Mauritians are a mix of African Creoles and small minorities of Chinese and French. This makes Mauritius unique among other Indian diasporas because in most contexts (e.g., Guyana, Trinidad, Fiji, South Africa) Indians are "confronted with a hegemonic national identity tending towards their exclusion" (Eisenlohr 2006: 28). Given this demographic landscape, Eisenlohr argues that Hindus maintain their religious tradition in this particular diaspora primarily through linguistic practices.

Little India turns on a puzzle that appears confusing at first glance. English is the official language of government and public education, a remnant of the British colonial rule that lasted until 1968. However, English is rarely used outside such formal institutional settings. French dominates as the language of the private sector economy, print media, and Mauritian-based television and radio. Bhojpuri, a north Indian language, is used in everyday conversation by 20–25 percent of the population, but always bilingually with a second language. The dominant language of everyday life, the language known by all Mauritians, is Mauritian Creole. This evolved from the mixing of African slaves and French settlers between 1715 and 1810. The puzzle is this: if Creole, Bhojpuri, French, and English are the languages that are actually in use on Mauritius, why does the state provide financial and political support to teach and promote Hindi, an Indian language "never used in everyday life" (31)?

The answer is what Eisenlohr calls "ethnolinguistic nationalism": the use of language as a symbol for belonging, dominance, and, ultimately, cultural purity. In the case of Mauritius, Hindi provides a durable connection to the Indian homeland and is treated as an "ancestral language." Where, then, is Hindi found in Mauritian life? It is primarily used in Hindu rituals: temple sermons and worship, festivals, and devotional events held in homes. Hindi is also taught to students of north Indian origin in state schools at every grade level and in supplemental courses that meet once a week. There is Hindi programming on state-controlled mass media. And, the state subsidizes Hindu organizations and Indian cultural centers that promote Hindi. Eisenlohr argues that "ancestral language emerges as a key element in the invention of official diasporic ancestral cultures" (6).

Part of this puzzle still lingers. Where does the political will come from that keeps the state deeply invested in Hindi? After all, only a slight majority (52 percent) are Hindu Indians. The answer is the political presence and influence of "a complex and dense Hindu nationalist network" (36) in Mauritius. Hindu nationalists promote an ideology of *hindutva* ("Hindu-ness"), which sees India as rightfully a Hindu nation and is highly critical of India's embrace of secular modernity and religious pluralism (see Chapters 2 and 4 for other examples of Hindu nationalism). The roots of *hindutva* stretch to the late 1800s, when anti-Muslim and anti-British Hindus fought for independence. Hindu nationalists see ancestral language as an irreplaceable resource: "Cultivating Hindi among Creole-speaking Hindus is thought to turn them into better and more committed Hindus in the diaspora" (46). So, in the case of Hindu Indians living on Mauritius, diasporic Hinduism is tethered to the linguistic vitality of Hindi. Note how well this example illustrates the holistic interconnections among religion, language, nationhood, belonging, migration history, and ethnic identity.

SECOND MIGRATION: WASHINGTON, D.C.

Our second example takes us to Washington, D.C., where the second global wave of Indian migration has created a community of approximately 40,000 Hindus. In the U.S. context, the post-1947 migration combined with a 1965 federal law abolishing a quota system for how many Asian migrants were allowed entry to the United States (a system that had been in place since the passing of a 1924 federal law). The result is a large Indian diaspora that is English-speaking, mostly urban, and well educated. In the D.C. suburb of Lanham, Maryland, the historian and ethnographer Joanne Waghorne (1999) did fieldwork at the Sri Siva-Vishnu Temple (SSVT). Sitting on 14 acres of suburban land, this is one of America's largest Hindu temples. Hindu priests living throughout the United States first gathered in Lanham to consecrate the SSVT in 1990. A multi-million dollar complex, SSVT reflects the middle-class and upwardly mobile demographic of most post-1947 Indian migrants.

Conducting fieldwork on a Hindu temple is a wise ethnographic decision, as temples are important sites for understanding diasporic Hinduism. The reason is that Hindu Gods "live in temples" (Waghorne 1999: 105) via a specialized consecration process. "Four-day *pranapratistha* rituals 'fix' (*pratistha*) the 'life breath' (*prana*) into the stone sculpture [of a God], transforming [the sculpture] from a work of art into a visible embodiment of a God" (112). Once the temple icons have been transformed, they must be regularly cared for with offerings. This ensures a constant presence of devotees at the temple sites. This presence serves as a foundational part of Hindu piety, which is grounded in an active relationship between devotees and deities (*darshana*). Through her research, Waghorne found that temple practices in the United States differed from those in India, revealing a form of religious change in the diaspora.

"Traditional temples in South India often house several deities" (118), but the amount of deity diversity at the SSVT is unprecedented in the homeland. D.C.-area devotees "chose to construct a temple that would unite the two major Hindu traditions, Vaishnavism and Shaivism, 'under one roof' ... Thus the Gods Siva and Vishnu are each housed in their own shrines" (117). Waghorne's consultants explained to her that the temple architecture was precisely engineered to "balance the two cosmic forces embodied" (ibid.) in these two

Gods. Like Eisenlohr, Waghorne confronted a puzzle. In her case, despite a grand effort to establish a united Hinduism, the temple design created a strict "separation of sacred from secular" (118). The SSVT's two main levels were divided according to practices marked as "social" and "ritual" in nature. "Music, eating, office work, and education are now 'downstairs' functions, while upstairs is reserved for the holy rituals and ceremonies" (ibid.). Waghorne argues that this logic of division is both inconsistent with traditional Hinduism and quite consistent with a popular American notion that religion is distinct from other aspects of life (e.g., work, leisure, politics).

If Eisenlohr's example shows us a case where diasporic Hinduism seeks to establish an unchanging connection with the homeland (via language), Waghorne's example shows us a case where diasporic Hinduism adapts homeland religious practice (temple building) to a new cultural context. In her case, religion in diaspora underwent some changes, which she understood through an analysis of architecture, materiality, and devotees' interaction with the built environment.

Box 6.2 French Islam as diasporic religion

In this section, we compared two examples of diasporic Hinduism. With this foundation, you can consider a different example and do some analysis of your own. For this exercise, reflect on the case study of North African Muslims living in France.

On October 27, 2005 civil unrest erupted in Paris. Eventually spreading to other French cities like Lyon and Toulouse, it began in Clichy-sous-Bois, an eastern Parisian *banlieue* (high-density, lower-income residential area). The unrest continued for three weeks: thousands of cars and buildings were burned, over 100 people were injured, nearly 3,000 were arrested, and the estimated damage was 200 million Euros. The tipping point on October 27 was the death of two teenagers, but tensions had been swelling for years. The *banlieues* are home to rampant unemployment, poverty, accusations of police brutality, and many, including Clichy-sous-Bois, are majority migrant communities.

Most of these migrants are North African (Algerian, Moroccan, and Tunisian), which means they share a colonial history with France. Morocco and Tunisia were protected states of France until 1956, and Algeria was a French colony from 1830 to 1962. To help rebuild the ravages of World War II, French government and industry imported male labor from colonial Algeria. As a result of this shared past, North African migrants in France feel both a sense of belonging (e.g., French is a first language for most) and a sense of exclusion and discrimination as a marked social Other. Along with their ethnic, national, and class differences from the majority population, most North African migrants are Muslim. France does not maintain a religious census, but there are an estimated four to five million Muslims in the country, 60–70 percent of whom are migrants (Bowen 2004).

The 2005 riots were *not* religiously motivated; they were about social and economic marginalization. But, part of the exclusion North African migrants experience in France derives from their religious identity. French secularism (*laïcité*) is the ruling political ideology, which translates to broader cultural norms that favor the privatization of religion. With their increased presence in France, North African Muslims have had to negotiate their piety with secular expectations. French public schools emerged as the most visible arena for this negotiation. In particular, female Muslim students have been asked to remove their veils (an important gendered symbol of piety and modesty) because veils are said to violate *laïcité* principles. The first school controversy occurred in northern France in 1989, and in 2004 a countrywide law was passed banning "ostentatious" religious symbols in public contexts (along with the Muslim *hijab* this includes Jewish yarmulkes and Sikh turbans) (Bowen 2004). As with the example of Hindus in Mauritius and Washington, D.C., migration histories matter greatly for understanding this case of diasporic religion.

This milieu of banned veils and violent unrest creates the social backdrop for everyday life among North African Muslims in France. To further your understanding of diasporic Islam in France, perform a comparative analysis of media reporting about the 2005 riots. Using an Internet search engine, find ten media texts (news reports, interviews, videos) about the riots from at least two different nations (e.g., the United States, Britain, Cameroon). Once you have your data cache of media texts, consider the following questions:

- How do these reports compare?
- Are the riots framed differently in different national media?
- Who is attributed agency in the riots and who is not? What kind of agency is attributed?
- How are migrants as a group and migration as a process represented?
- How is Islam represented?
- Taken together, how does this media analysis help you understand diasporic religion?

TRANSNATIONAL RELIGION

Diasporic religion is one expression of the problem of religious globalization. In this section, we take up a second expression: religions that exist transnationally. What distinguishes a religion that has successfully secured a transnational presence? First, they operate via transnational networks of institutions, media (print, electronic, and virtual), symbol systems, and (in some cases) charismatic leaders. These networks connect individuals and groups who are separated geographically, ensuring a constant circulation of cultural content and enabling people to envision themselves as part of a global religious community. Second, transnational religions are continually localized. As they enter new places, local communities engage transnational religions in various ways; from mass conversion to selectively resisting, challenging, and adapting elements of the religious system. The process of localization is especially revealing because it reiterates a central question of globalization studies: is a globalized world one of increasing sameness or increasing fragmentation?

To illustrate some dynamics of transnational religion, we will consider the case of Rastafarianism gone global. As we work through two ethnographic examples, you can return to a few questions raised by this brief introduction. Which elements of a transnational network are visible (institutions, media, symbols, charismatic leaders) and what kinds of cultural content are being circulated? How does the consciousness of being part of a global religious community impact religious identity and practice? What are the mechanisms of localization? And, how does the process of localization unfold; is there change, continuity, tension between the local and the transnational network?

GLOBAL RASTAS

From its 1931 beginning, in the economically distraught island slums of Kingston, Jamaica, Rastafarianism has become a global religion in less than a half century. We might even say that Rastafari was always well fated to be a transnational religious movement because one of its organizing doctrines is repatriation to the claimed homeland of Ethiopia.

Outside of Jamaica, Rastafarianism first gained traction on other Caribbean islands. The Rastas' outspoken critique of capitalism, exploitation, and racial oppression resounded among former colonized nations and "corrupt and inefficient neoliberal Caribbean societies" (Savishinsky 1994: 262). In some cases, Rastas have been on the frontlines of Caribbean social and political upheaval; such as the participation of more than 400 Rastas in the March 1979 overthrow of the Grenadian government. Rastafarianism focuses on pan-African racial unity, and because of this it has emerged as "one of the most visible, potent, and progressive pan-regional cultural forces ... breaking down the many inter-island and inter-ethnic rivalries that have polarized [the Caribbean] for centuries" (263).

Between 1955 and 1962 some 200,000 Jamaicans immigrated to Britain, many of whom brought their Rastafarianism with them (265). On at least two occasions, 1958 and 1981, race riots in British cities produced a rapid growth in Rasta communities. By the late 1970s, there were thriving Rasta communities in other major European urban centers, including Birmingham, Amsterdam, and Paris. Outside Western Europe, Rasta communities have been in Ethiopia, Ghana, Gambia, Sierra Leone, Nigeria, Zimbabwe, South Africa, Australia, and New Zealand since the early 1970s.

Here we have another puzzle: how do we explain the global success of a movement that is recent in origin, motivated by racial dilemmas, notoriously informal in group organization, and popular among marginalized groups with few resources to mobilize? In a review of global Rastafarianism, anthropologist Neil Savishinsky (1994) offers six reasons, several of which recall Csordas' maxim of "transposability":

- the central role of the Christian Bible lends the movement familiarity;
- emphasizing all-natural nutrition and medicine resonates with various health movements;
- the vehement critique of colonial and post-colonial inequalities attracts other marginalized groups and those sympathetic with this critique;
- venerating African and indigenous ancestry appeals to non-whites;
- the informal group organization is actually helpful for spreading the movement because it allows for a great deal of flexibility when localizing;
- and, Rastafarianism travels with other forms of transnational popular culture (namely, the music of global icon Bob Marley).

Savishinsky places the greatest weight on this last reason: "it has been reggae music which has functioned as the primary catalyst for spreading the religion and culture of Rastafari beyond its original island homeland" (261). We might add two other reasons to Savishinsky's list:

- the local, regional, and global changes that have negatively impacted national economies in Africa and the Caribbean produced continuous waves of emigrants;
- the highly portable symbol system used by Rastas, including lion figures, dreadlocks, red–green–gold color combinations, and images of Haile Selassie and Bob Marley (recall Csordas' maxim of "portability").

Consider Savishinsky's six reasons, as well as these two, as we look closely at two case studies of global Rastafarianism.

BROOKLYN RASTAS

We begin in New York City, with The Church of Haile Selassie I (CHSI). This example comes from the work of Randal Hepner (1998), a sociologist and ethnographer of American religions. The CHSI was started by Abuna (Father) Asento Foxe, who began as a charismatic Rastafari leader in the 1950s. Born in Depression-era Kingston, Foxe moved to England in 1955 and started the first Rasta community in London following the 1958 Notting Hill race riots. In 1974 a military coup overthrew the Ethiopian monarchy and led to the arrest and death (Foxe would say "murder") of Haile Selassie. How to interpret this coup immediately became a dividing point among Rastas. Some, like Foxe, believed the coup was antithetical to the Rastafari worldview and aspirations, and formally denounced the new Ethiopian regime. Foxe returned to Jamaica where he "developed into a prolific composer of Rasta diatribes published as letters to the editor in Jamaica's leading newspapers" (Hepner 1998: 206). In many of these critiques Foxe targeted other Rasta communities for not joining him in denouncing the coup against Selassie.

Throughout the late 1970s and early 1980s Foxe rallied with other like-minded Rastas. In 1987 he founded the first CHSI in Kingston. In 1990 he moved to New York City and in 1994 the North American branch of the CHSI began in the Brooklyn neighborhood of Bedford-Stuyvesant (Bed-Stuy), home to many West Indian migrants. During Hepner's fieldwork, the church's membership was constant but transient and reflected the neighborhood demographics: a mix of Afro-Caribs (from Trinidad, Barbados, Grenada, Guyana, Haiti, and St. Lucia), Puerto Ricans, African-Americans, and a few whites.

In this North American localization, Hepner observed several important changes from traditional Rastafarianism. First, in forming as a congregation the CHSI adopted the primary institutional form of North American religious life. Being organized congregationally is markedly different from the largely informal and decentralized pattern that has historically characterized Rasta communities. Second, the Rastafari movement traditionally focuses on African-descent communities and repatriation (literal and symbolic) to Ethiopia. The CHSI diverges in being an evangelizing organization with a global consciousness. This is expressed in several ways. Along with New York City, Foxe sent Rasta leaders to start CHSI branches in London, Paris, the Netherlands, and St. Lucia. This missionizing approach includes "training" new leaders, a practice that is foreign among traditional Rastafarians who "scorned professional Christian ministers and the very concept of a 'learned clergy'" (Hepner 1998: 209). Foxe also led evangelizing efforts in North America, most visibly by starting a prison ministry in which he is a paid chaplain of the New York State Correctional System. The third major change pertains to gender roles. Since the earliest social science accounts of Rastas in the 1960s, the movement has been labeled as patriarchal, focusing on men to such an extent that women were deemed "peripheral" (216). In the life of the CHSI, this seems to be changing as "sisters … emphasize the necessity of women taking responsibility for their own spiritual and educational development" (215). One way women mark this change of status in public settings is through naming. The traditional gendered term, "Rastawoman," is explicitly replaced with "Daughter of Zion" as a critique of female subordination and an empowerment of female legitimation rooted in scripture.

JAPANESE RASTAS

From Brooklyn we go to Japan, with Marvin Sterling's ethnography *Babylon East* (2010). Sterling did fieldwork with Japanese men and women who interweave various forms of Jamaican popular culture into their musical and spiritual lives. Among them, Sterling found a small, but vibrant Rasta network. Finding Japanese Rastas is a profound testament to the globalizing capacity of this religion because we see an Afro-centric movement being taken up by non-Africans (not to mention a Caribbean movement being taken up in the Far East). Like Savishinsky, Sterling argues that Rastafarianism transcends ethnic differences because it appeals to moral and spiritual concerns about alienation and oppression that extend beyond racial identity.

From April 5 to 13, 1979, Bob Marley and the Wailers played five concerts in Tokyo and two in Osaka. It was the group's first and only trip to Japan. This event, which continues to live as "legendary" (Sterling 2010: 10) in fans' collective memory, was a catalyst for both devotees of reggae music and Rasta practitioners. Among the latter, Sterling discovered through his fieldwork that there is one major divide in how Rastafarianism has localized in Japan: there are major differences between urban and rural practitioners. Japan's urban Rastas closely mirror our iconic notions of Rastafarianism: they emphasize the perils of Babylon (alive in the Japanese East and abroad in the West), colonial and post-colonial regimes of exploitation, class inequalities, and the spiritual dangers of consumer capitalism. When Sterling takes us into the room of a 37-year-old Dread named Taz we are in a scene familiar to Rastas around the globe: walls covered with images of Haile Selassie I, Bob Marley, the Dalai Lama, Karl Marx, Che Guevera, Friedrich Engels, and Vladimir Lenin.

Japan's rural Rastas also perform the traditional Rastafarian spiritual critique of Babylon's socio-political inequality, but they place a far greater emphasis on the spiritual importance of communing with nature. Ideologically, they position the rural as the positive spiritual counterpoint to the urban, the seat of Babylon's oppression, cosmopolitanism, capitalist consumption, and political corruption. They say the Japanese countryside is where the spiritual promise of Rastafarianism can be fulfilled. Sterling argues that this difference among rural Rastas makes sense in light of two Japanese cultural traditions. First, Buddhists and Shintos both venerate ideals of rural, unspoiled nature. In fact, many of the rural Rastas Sterling interviewed were either disaffected Buddhists or Shintos. Second, rural Japan has a history of counterculture movements, all of which combine "into one big stew everything considered ethnic" (167). In other words, there is already in place a cultural impetus to buck the Japanese mainstream and connect with a global ethnic Other. This primed the local pump for accepting Rasta ideology and aesthetics.

Having considered these two examples, reflect on the eight reasons we discussed above for explaining the global reach of Rastafarianism. Which reasons are evident in the examples from Brooklyn (Hepner) and Japan (Sterling)? Does one or a select few reasons seem to have more explanatory power? Why? Would you add to the list of eight reasons, or subtract any from the list, based on these examples?

Box 6.3 Charismatic Christianity as transnational religion

To conclude this section, you can think closely about another example of transnational religion. This example far exceeds Rastafarianism in terms of the number of adherents the religious movement claims and the extent of the movement's global reach. Since the 1920s, charismatic Christianity has been the fastest growing religion in the world. The question we will work up to is this: What explanations have anthropologists put forward to account for this story of global religious success? First, we need some demographic and historical context.

In 2006, the Pew Research Center published the findings from a large-scale demographic survey. The results include the following, rather staggering, results. At least a quarter of the world's two billion Christians (c.500 million people) are now Pentecostals or charismatics (we'll say more about this terminological difference below). Over half live in the Global South: more than 150 million in Latin America and more than 100 million in Africa. In some nations, Pentecostals or charismatics account for more than a quarter of the total population: Nigeria (26 percent), Chile (30 percent), South Africa (34 percent), Philippines (44 percent), Brazil (49 percent), Kenya (56 percent), and Guatemala (60 percent).

So, who are charismatic Christians? What distinguishes them? Like many evangelical Christians, charismatics invest high value in an individual born-again conversion experience, converting non-Christians, claim the Bible as their ultimate authority, and rely on a biblically based moral framework to guide everyday life. Scholars of religion typically distinguish charismatics by two sets of practices. First, charismatics emphasize, to borrow some biblical language, "gifts of the Holy Spirit." Perhaps the most notable is speaking in tongues but charismatics recognize numerous other gifts, from healing to receiving prophetic revelation directly from God, and exorcizing demonic spirits. Second, charismatic Christianity is a deeply visceral tradition; everyday and ritual contexts emphasize whole-body experiences, from multi-sensory modes of attention to dancing, singing, touching, and praying aloud. The difference between charismatics and Pentecostals is often in name only, though the substance of the difference can vary quite a bit from one local context to another. An easy way to think about it is this: Pentecostals are charismatics who belong to a denomination or organization that formally declares gifts of the Spirit to be a central part of identity. All Pentecostals are charismatic, but not all charismatics are Pentecostal.

Most histories of the modern charismatic movement set its birth in the United States, during the opening years of the 20th century. Beginning in locations like Topeka, Kansas, and Houston, Texas, the standard story takes us to Bonnie Brae Street in central Los Angeles. There, on April 9, 1906, a small fellowship who had been praying to receive the gift of tongues for several days finally received that gift. Several months later they moved into a former church building, two miles away, on Asuza Street. Hundreds joined the original fellowship and they began doing round-the-clock revival worship. This period is known as the Asuza Street Revival. Much like the early Rastas in Kingston, Jamaica, charismatic Christianity began among a small group of relatively poor people, marginalized from the mainstream of their society.

The movement became transnational soon after its start, with missionaries leaving directly from the streets of southern California (Maxwell 2007). Asuza Street also led to the formation in 1914 of the Assemblies of God, now the World Assemblies of God Fellowship. This is the largest Pentecostal denomination with churches in 212 nations and more than 65 million members. Other major Pentecostal denominations have arisen outside the United States, such as the Redeemed Christian Church of God in Nigeria in 1952 and the Universal Church of the Kingdom of God in Brazil in 1977. These latter two denominations reflect what some call neo-Pentecostalism, which adds an official teaching that God desires true believers to be prosperous on earth as well as in heaven. (This growing segment of global charismatic Christianity is variously called "prosperity theology," "the Faith movement," or "the health and wealth gospel," and has its roots in the radio and television ministries ("televangelism") that became popular in the United States in the 1950s.)

In short, from 1900 to 2006, this religious movement went from being practiced by a few hundred individuals in Los Angeles to being 500 million strong. How? This is a question that anthropologists of Christianity have wrestled with. An easy answer might simply highlight the zealous missionary aspect of the movement. But, there are plenty of missionary religions, equally zealous, that have experienced minor gains or declining memberships. There is also no central institutional entity or charismatic persona that explains the movement's global reach. There is no single site where strategy is coordinated and materials produced, and no single individual to trace success to. Consider, then, four possible explanations. After reading each, ask yourself how compelling the explanation is, what makes sense about it, and if you are suspicious of any portion.

- *The critical approach.* This explanation links the success of Pentecostalism directly to socio-economic conditions of poverty and global marginality. Because so much charismatic growth has happened in the Global South, and because larger numbers of adherents live economically poor or uncertain lives, some scholars see Pentecostalism primarily as a means to confront economic stress. This is partly about a theological basis for accepting one's circumstances as they are, but it is also about a religious logic for affirming and pursuing the promise of upward mobility. Due to its American origins, some scholars see Pentecostal conversion as a kind of neo-colonialism, where conversion is about modernization and merely a step removed from American imperialism. For a version of this approach applied ethnographically, see Andrew Chestnut's *Born Again in Brazil* (1997).
- *The structural approach.* This explanation contextualizes the accelerated growth of Pentecostalism in the last quarter of the 20th century within the global neoliberal shift, in which national and transnational actors have adopted a political–economic ideology that focuses on privatization. As the public sector recedes due to neoliberal state reforms, and formerly public services increasingly became privately run, a need develops for volunteer institutions to fill the gaps left open. Churches, and in particular large

megachurches like those common among neo-Pentecostals, become institutions that fill those gaps. For example, if you lack health care and/or access to a hospital, charismatic healing becomes all the more attractive and necessary. Along with this privatization dynamic, neo-Pentecostalism's focus on individual salvation and self-care resonates with neoliberal capitalism's focus on individual responsibility (and vice versa). This is not a cause–effect explanation, in which neoliberal shifts trigger spikes in charismatic memberships. It is more about these two systems sharing an elective affinity; they favor and are favored by one another. For a version of this approach applied ethnographically, see Kevin Lewis O'Neill's *City of God* (2010), a study of a neo-charismatic megachurch in Guatemala City.

- *The ritual approach.* This explanation moves the focus away from the social conditions that engulf global Pentecostalism and relocates the focus to a core feature of Pentecostal religion itself. In this approach, Pentecostalism has globalized so successfully because it provides a ritual-filled institutional life that is easily recognizable, easily learned, and easily practiced. The non-verbal (sensorial and embodied) nature of Pentecostal ritual has the nice function of transcending linguistic barriers. New converts can develop ritual expertise with relative ease, and transplants or visiting preachers from other churches can seamlessly participate in local ritual life. Even after a local church has fully adapted Pentecostalism to its context, it is still familiar as an expression of the same charismatic Christianity you find elsewhere. It is ritual that makes Pentecostalism a moveable, translatable, transposable, and portable religion. For a cogent theoretical outline of this approach, see Joel Robbins' essay "Pentecostal Networks and the Spirit of Globalization" (2009).

- *The cultural approach.* This explanation elaborates on the basic idea of the Ritual approach; that there is something about the nature of charismatic Christianity enabling it to successfully move from place to place. Here, the explanation goes beyond ritual to encompass a range of charismatic cultural practices and logics. Charismatic Christianity offers a definable, internally coherent cultural system that can be replicated in limitless contexts. For example, there is the neo-Pentecostal language ideology of "positive confession," in which charismatics name the prosperity they want God to provide in their lives as a first step toward achieving that prosperity. Or, there is the gift economy of sacrificial giving, in which charismatics tithe gifts to the church in order to make themselves available to be receivers of gifts from God. For a version of this approach applied ethnographically, see Simon Coleman's *The Globalisation of Charismatic Christianity* (2000), a study of a neo-charismatic megachurch in Uppsala, Sweden.

Which explanation is most compelling to you? Why? Did you note any suspicions as you were reading? After gathering your thoughts and notes, reflect on four questions:

- We need not treat these four explanations as mutually exclusive. We can find merit in each. Are there ways in which you find these explanations complementary? Could they be combined to explain different aspects of Pentecostalism's successful globalization?
- How do these explanations for Pentecostalism as a transnational religion compare to those we considered for global Rastafarianism? As anthropological approaches, do they highlight similar or different processes?
- Recall the work we did in this chapter's opening section on definitions of globalization. How do these explanations for global Pentecostalism resonate with those definitions and the observations we made about them?
- In the section "Ethnoscapes, meet sacroscapes," we used the work of Paul Johnson and Thomas Csordas to outline four reasons why religion travels well. Johnson proposed that religious identity survives the disruptive process of mobility, and that mobility draws out the social and affective power of religious belonging. Csordas proposed the dual qualities of portable practice and transposable message. How do the Critical, Structural, Ritual, and Cultural explanations engage with these four observations? Are there any that are left unaddressed?

CHAPTER SUMMARY

In this chapter, we explored the various relationships that exist between global formations and religious worlds. We began by discussing anthropological definitions of globalization. From there, we introduced the term sacroscapes as a way to link religion with a defining feature of globalization, "flows." We then distinguished two expressions of religious globalization: diasporic religion and transnational religion. For the former, we asked how religion that is practiced in diasporic cultures might be a distinctive kind of religious culture. For the latter, we asked how to explain the successful spread of religious systems across national, ethnic, linguistic, and cultural boundaries. Along the way, we relied on a number of ethnographic examples to guide us. We considered:

- The Virgin of Guadalupe as a transnational symbol;
- Indian Hindus living on the island of Mauritius and in Washington, D.C.;
- North African Muslims in Paris, France;
- Rastafarians in New York City and Japan;
- The globalization of charismatic Christianity.

Ultimately, this chapter helps us think about the way religious systems, identities, and practices exist and change in global contexts. Globalization is not purely an economic phenomenon; it includes various forms of cultural globalization. Religion is a prime example, and an important task for the anthropology of religion is to continue asking great questions about how religion is an accelerating global force (alongside and in tension with other transnational systems, such as neoliberal capitalism). I hope this chapter has provided some useful examples to think with and some useful ways to conceptualize religious globalization. If you are doing original research or fieldwork for your class, how are global and transnational dynamics relevant to your project?

SUGGESTIONS FOR FURTHER READING

In addition to the works cited in this chapter, the following books and essays are productive places to go next. To follow up on

"Religious globalization," Robert Hefner's review essay "Multiple Modernities: Christianity, Islam, and Hinduism in a Globalizing Age" (*Annual Review of Anthropology*, 1998) is insightful. *Religion, Politics, and Globalization: Anthropological Approaches* (Berghahn 2011) gathers ten theoretical and ethnographic essays. For "Religion in diaspora," Paul Christopher Johnson's review essay "Religion and Diaspora" (*Advances in Research: Religion and Society*, 2012) is helpful. *Gatherings in Diaspora: Religious Communities and the New Immigration* (Temple University Press, 1998) features 12 ethnographic essays focused on diasporic religion in the United States. To continue exploring "Transnational religion," the edited volume *Transnational Transcendence: Essays on Religion and Globalization* (University of California Press, 2009) gathers 13 provocative contributions. For an ethnography of a religious community spread globally, there is *Spirits without Borders: Vietnamese Spirit Mediums in a Transnational Age* (Palgrave Macmillan, 2011).

BIBLIOGRAPHY

Appadurai, Arjun. 1996. *Modernity at Large: Cultural Dimensions of Globalization.* Minneapolis, MN: University of Minnesota Press.

Asad, Talal. 1993. *Genealogies of Religion: Discipline and Reasons of Power in Christianity and Islam.* Baltimore, MD: Johns Hopkins University Press.

——2003. *Formations of the Secular: Christianity, Islam, Modernity.* Stanford, CA: Stanford University Press.

Atran, Scott. 2002. *In Gods We Trust: The Evolutionary Landscape of Religion.* New York and Oxford: Oxford University Press.

Austin, J.L. 1962. *How to Do Things with Words.* New York and Oxford: Oxford University Press.

Bado-Fralick, Nikki and Rebecca Sachs Norris. 2010. *Toying with God: The World of Religious Games and Dolls.* Baylor, TX: Baylor University Press.

Badone, Ellen and Sharon R. Roseman, eds. 2004. *Intersecting Journeys: The Anthropology of Pilgrimage and Tourism.* Urbana-Champaign, IL: University of Illinois Press.

Bauman, Richard. 1974. 'Speaking in the Light: The Role of the Quaker Minister.' In *Explorations in the Ethnography of Speaking.* Richard Bauman and Joel Sherzer, eds. pp. 144–62. Cambridge: Cambridge University Press.

Bell, Catherine. 1992. *Ritual Theory, Ritual Practice.* New York and Oxford: Oxford University Press.

——1997. *Ritual: Perspectives and Dimensions.* New York and Oxford: Oxford University Press.

Bennion, Janet. 2011a. 'History, Culture, and Variability of Mormon Schismatic Groups.' In *Modern Polygamy in the United States: Historical, Legal, and Cultural*

Issues. Cardell K. Jacobson with Lara Burton, eds. pp. 101–24. New York and Oxford: Oxford University Press.

——2011b. 'The Many Faces of Polygamy: An Analysis of the Variability in Modern Mormon Fundamentalism in the Intermountain West.' In *Modern Polygamy in the United States: Historical, Legal, and Cultural Issues*. Cardell K. Jacobson with Lara Burton, eds. pp. 163–84. New York and Oxford: Oxford University Press.

Berger, Peter. 1967. *The Sacred Canopy: Elements of a Sociological Theory of Religion*. New York: Anchor Books.

Berger, Peter and Thomas Luckmann. 1966. *The Social Construction of Reality: A Treatise in the Sociology of Knowledge*. New York: Anchor Books.

Bialecki, Jon. 2014. Does God Exist in Methodological Atheism? On Tanya Luhrmann's *When God Talks Back* and Bruno Latour. *Anthropology of Consciousness* 25(1): 32–52.

Bielo, James S. 2009. *Words upon the Word: An Ethnography of Evangelical Group Bible Study*. New York: NYU Press.

——2011. *Emerging Evangelicals: Faith, Modernity, and Authenticity*. New York: NYU Press.

——2013. Doing Religious Studies Dialogically. *Practical Matters: A Transdisciplinary Multimedia Journal of Religious Practices and Practical Theology* (6): 1–6.

Bourdieu, Pierre. 1977. *Outline of a Theory of Practice*. Cambridge: Cambridge University Press.

Bowen, John. 1993. *Muslims through Discourse: Religion and Ritual in Gayo Society*. Princeton, NJ: Princeton University Press.

——2004. *Religions in Practice: An Approach to the Anthropology of Religion*. New York: Pearson.

Bowie, Fiona. 2000. *The Anthropology of Religion*. London: Blackwell.

Bowman, Glenn. 1991. 'Christian Ideology and the Image of a Holy Land: the Place of Jerusalem Pilgrimage in the Various Christianities.' In *Contesting the Sacred: The Anthropology of Christian Pilgrimage*. John Eade and Michael Sallnow, eds. London: Routledge.

——1993. Nationalizing the Sacred: Shrines and Shifting Identities in the Israeli-Occupied Territories. *Man* 28(3): 431–60.

Boyer, Pascal. 2001. *Religion Explained: The Evolutionary Origins of Religious Thought*. New York: Basic Books.

Brown, Karen McCarthy. 1991. *Mama Lola: A Vodou Priestess in Brooklyn*. Berkeley, CA: University of California Press.

——2002. 'Writing about "the Other," Revisited.' In *Personal Knowledge and Beyond: Reshaping the Ethnography of Religion*. James V. Spickard, J. Shawn Landres, and Meredith B. McGuire, eds. New York: NYU Press.

Burdick, John. 2013. *The Color of Sound: Race, Religion, and Music in Brazil*. New York: NYU Press.

Butler, Ella. 2010. God Is in the Data: Epistemologies of Knowledge at the Creation Museum. *Ethnos* 75(3): 229–51.

Butler, Jon. 2010. 'Disquieted History in *A Secular Age*.' In *Varieties of Secularism in a Secular Age*. Michael Warner, Jonathan VanAntwerpen, and Craig Calhoun, eds. pp. 193–216. Cambridge, MA: Harvard University Press.

Cahn, Peter S. 2008. Consuming Class: Multilevel Marketers in Neoliberal Mexico. *Cultural Anthropology* 23(3): 429–52.

——2011. *Direct Sales and Direct Faith in Latin America*. New York: Palgrave Macmillan.

Calabrese, Joseph. 2013. *A Different Medicine: Postcolonial Healing in the Native American Church*. New York and Oxford: Oxford University Press.

Cannell, Fenella. 2013. The Blood of Abraham: Mormon Redemptive Physicality and American Idioms of Kinship. *Journal of the Royal Anthropological Institute* 19(s1): s77–s94.

Carter, Lewis F. 1990. *Charisma and Control in Rajneeshpuram: A Community without Shared Values*. Cambridge: Cambridge University Press.

Casanova, Jose. 1994. *Public Religions in the Modern World*. Chicago: University of Chicago Press.

Chestnut, Andrew. 1997. *Born Again in Brazil: The Pentecostal Boom and the Pathogens of Poverty*. New Brunswick, NJ: Rutgers University Press.

Chidester, David and Edward T. Linenthal, eds. 1995. *American Sacred Space*. Bloomington, IN: Indiana University Press.

Clifford, James and George Marcus, eds. 1986. *Writing Culture: The Poetics and Politics of Ethnography*. Berkeley, CA: University of California Press.

Coleman, Simon. 2000. *The Globalisation of Charismatic Christianity: Spreading the Gospel of Prosperity*. Cambridge: Cambridge University Press.

——2002a. Do You Believe in Pilgrimage? From *Communitas* to Contestation and Beyond. *Anthropological Theory* 2(3): 355–68.

——2002b. '"But Are They Really Christian?" Contesting Knowledge and Identity in and out of the Field.' In *Personal Knowledge and Beyond: Reshaping the Ethnography of Religion*. James V. Spickard, J. Shawn Landres, and Meredith B. McGuire, eds. New York: NYU Press.

——2006. 'When Silence Isn't Golden: Charismatic Speech and the Limits of Literalism.' In *The Limits of Meaning: Case Studies in the Anthropology of Christianity*. Matt Tomlinson and Matthew Engelke, eds. pp. 39–61. Oxford: Berghahn.

Coleman, Simon and Leslie Carlin, eds. 2004. *The Cultures of Creationism: Anti-evolutionism in English Speaking Countries*. London: Ashgate.

Corr, Rachel. 2004. To Throw the Blessing: Poetics, Prayer, and Performance in the Andes. *The Journal of Latin American and Caribbean Anthropology* 9(2): 382–408.

Crane, Hillary. 2013. 'Flirting with Conversion: Negotiating Researcher Non-Belief with Missionaries.' In *Missionary Impositions: Conversion, Resistance, and Other Challenges to Objectivity in Religious Ethnography*. Hillary K. Crane and Deana Weibel, eds. pp. 11–24. Lanham, MD: Lexington Books.

Csordas, Thomas. 2009. 'Modalities of Transnational Transcendence.' In *Transnational Transcendence: Essays on Religion and Globalization*. Thomas Csordas, ed. pp. 1–29. Berkeley, CA: University of California Press.

D'Alisera, JoAnn. 2004. *An Imagined Geography: Sierra Leonean Muslims in America*. Philadelphia, PA: University of Pennsylvania Press.

Danforth, Loring M. 1989. *Firewalking and Religious Healing: The Anastenaria of Greece and the American Firewalking Movement*. Princeton, NJ: Princeton University Press.

Davidof, Veronica. 2010. Shamans and Shams: The Discursive Effects of Ethnotourism in Ecuador. *The Journal of Latin American and Caribbean Anthropology* 15(2): 387–410.

Delaney, Carole. 1990. The Hajj: Sacred and Secular. *American Ethnologist* 513–30.

Douglas, Mary. 1966. *Purity and Danger*. London: Routledge.

Droogers, Andres. 1996. 'Methodological Ludism: Beyond Religionism and Reductionism.' In *Conflicts in Social Science*. Anton van Harskamp, ed. pp. 44–67. London: Routledge.

——1999. 'The Third Bank of the River: Play, Methodological Ludism and the Definition of Religion.' In *The Pragmatics of Defining Religion: Contexts, Concepts, and Contents*. J.G. Platvoet and A.L. Molendijk, eds. pp. 285–313. Leiden: Brill.

Dubisch, Jill. 1995. *In a Different Place: Pilgrimage, Gender, and Politics at a Greek Island Shrine*. Princeton, NJ: Princeton University Press.

Dunstan, Adam. 2010. 'With Anything Manmade There Is Going to Be Danger': The Cultural Context of Navajo Opinions Regarding Snowmaking on the San Francisco Peaks. *Indigenous Policy Journal* 21(2): 1–6.

Durkheim, Emile. 1912. *The Elementary Forms of Religious Life*. New York: Free Press.

Dwyer, Kevin. 1982. *Moroccan Dialogues: Anthropology in Question*. Long Grove, IL: Waveland Press.

Eade, John and Michael J. Sallnow, eds. 1991. *Contesting the Sacred: The Anthropology of Christian Pilgrimage*. Urbana-Champaign, IL: University of Illinois Press.

Ebron. 2000. Tourists as Pilgrims: Commercial Fashioning of Transatlantic Politics. *American Ethnologist* 26(4): 910–32.

Edelman, Marc and Angelique Haugerud. 2005. 'The Anthropology of Development and Globalization.' In *The Anthropology of Development and Globalization: From Classical Political Economy to Contemporary Neoliberalism*. Marc Edelman and Angelique Haugerud, eds. pp. 1–74. London: Blackwell.

Eisenlohr, Patrick. 2006. *Little India: Diaspora, Time, and Ethnolinguistic Belonging in Hindu Mauritius*. Berkeley, CA: University of California Press.

Engelke, Matthew. 2002. The Problem of Belief: Evans-Pritchard and Victor Turner on the 'Inner Life.' *Anthropology Today* 8(6): 3–8.

——2007. *A Problem of Presence: Beyond Scripture in an African Church*. Berkeley, CA: University of California Press.

——2010. Religion and the Media Turn: A Review Essay. *American Ethnologist* 37(2): 371–9.

——2013. *God's Agents: Biblical Publicity in Contemporary England*. Berkeley, CA: University of California Press.

Erez, Tamir. 2013. 'Mission Not Accomplished: Negotiating Power Relations and Vulnerability among Messianic Jews in Israel.' In *Ethnographic Encounters in Israel: Poetics and Ethics of Fieldwork*. Fran Markowitz, ed. pp. 40–58. Bloomington, IN: Indiana University Press.

Evans-Pritchard, E.E. 1937. *Witchcraft, Oracles, and Magic among the Azande*. New York and Oxford: Oxford University Press.

——1965. *Theories of Primitive Religion*. Westport, CT: Greenwood Press.

Ewing, Katherine. 1994. Dreams from a Saint: Anthropological Atheism and the Temptation to Believe. *American Anthropologist* 96(3): 571–83.

Fader, Ayala. 2009. *Mitzvah Girls: Bringing up the Next Generation of Hasidic Jews in Brooklyn*. Princeton, NJ: Princeton University Press.

Falcone, Jessica. 2012. Putting the 'Fun' in Fundamentalism: Religious Nationalism and the Split Self at Hindutva Summer Camps in the United States. *Ethos* 40(2): 164–95.

Farrer, Claire R. 1994. *Thunder Rides a Black Horse: Mescalero Apaches and the Mythic Present*. Long Grove, IL: Waveland Press.

Feld, Steven and Keith H. Basso. eds. 1996a. *Senses of Place*. Albuquerque, NM: School of American Research Press.

——1996b. 'Introduction.' *Senses of Place*. Steven Feld and Keith H. Basso, eds. pp. 3–12. Albuquerque, NM: School of American Research Press.

Field, Margaret and Taft Blackhorse, Jr. 2002. The Dual Role of Metonymy in Navajo Prayer. *Anthropological Linguistics* 44(3): 217–30.

Frazer, James. 1890 [1994]. *The Golden Bough: A Study in Magic and Religion*. New York and Oxford: Oxford University Press.

Freud, Sigmund. 1907 [1995]. 'Obsessive Actions and Religious Practices.' In *The Freud Reader*. Peter Gay, ed. New York: Norton.

——1913. *Totem and Taboo*. New York: Norton.

——1927. *The Future of an Illusion*. New York: Norton.

——1937. *Moses and Monotheism*. New York: Vintage.

Galvez, Alyshia. 2009. *Guadalupe in New York: Devotion and the Struggle for Citizenship Rights among Mexican Immigrants*. New York: NYU Press.

Geertz, Clifford. 1966. 'Religion as a Cultural System.' In *Anthropological Approaches to the Study of Religion*. Michael Banton, ed. pp. 1–46. London: Tavistock.

Giddens, Anthony. 1990. *The Consequences of Modernity*. Stanford, CA: Stanford University Press.

Gilbert, James. 1997. *Redeeming Culture: American Religion in an Age of Science*. Chicago: University of Chicago Press.

Gill, Sam. 1980. *Sacred Words: A Study of Navajo Religion and Prayer*. Westport, CT: Greenwood Press.

Glick-Schiller, Nina, *et al.* 2006. Beyond the Ethnic Lens: Locality, Globality, and Born-Again Incorporation. *American Ethnologist* 33(4): 612–33.

Goldman, Marion S. 1999. *Passionate Journeys: Why Successful Women Joined a Cult*. Ann Arbor, MI: University of Michigan Press.

——2002. 'Voicing Spiritualities: Anchored Composites as an Approach to Understanding Religious Commitment.' In *Personal Knowledge and Beyond: Reshaping the Ethnography of Religion*. James V. Spickard, J. Shawn Landres, and Meredith B. McGuire, eds. New York: NYU Press.

Gole, Nilufer. 2010. 'The Civilizational, Spatial, and Sexual Powers of the Secular.' In *Varieties of Secularism in a Secular Age*. Michael Warner, Jonathan VanAntwerpen, and Craig Calhoun, eds. pp. 243–64. Cambridge, MA: Harvard University Press.

Goluboff, Sascha. 2003. *Jewish Russians: Upheavals in a Moscow Synagogue*. Philadelphia, PA: University of Pennsylvania Press.

——2011. Making African American Homeplaces in Rural Virginia. *Ethos* 39(3): 368–94.

Gordon, David F. 1987. Getting Close by Staying Distant: Fieldwork with Proselytizing Groups. *Qualitative Sociology* 10(3): 267–87.

Gottlieb, Alma. 2004. *The Afterlife Is Where We Come From*. Chicago: University of Chicago Press.

Goulet, Jean-Guy A. 1994. Ways of Knowing: Towards a Narrative Ethnography of Experience among the Dene Tha. *Journal of Anthropological Research* 50(2): 113–39.

Graburn, Nelson H.H. 2004. 'The Kyoto Tax Strike: Buddhism, Shinto, and Tourism in Japan.' In *Intersecting Journeys: The Anthropology of Pilgrimage and Tourism*. Ellen Badone and Sharon R. Roseman, eds. pp. 125–39. Urbana-Champaign, IL: University of Illinois Press.

Guyer, Jane. 2007. Prophecy and the Near Future: Thoughts on Macroeconomic, Evangelical, and Punctuated Time. *American Ethnologist* 34(3): 409–21.

Harding, Susan F. 2000. *The Book of Jerry Falwell: Fundamentalist Language and Politics*. Princeton, NJ: Princeton University Press.

Hepner, Randal. 1998. 'The House that Rasta Built: Church-Building and Fundamentalism among New York Rastafarians.' In *Gatherings in Diaspora:*

Religious Communities and the New Immigration. R. Stephen Warner and Judith G. Wittner, eds. pp. 197–234. Philadelphia, PA: Temple University Press.

Horton, Robin. 1967. African Traditional Thought and Western Science. *Africa: Journal of the International African Institute* 37(1): 50–71.

Howell, Brian. 2007. The Repugnant Cultural Other Speaks Back: Christian Identity as Ethnographic 'Standpoint.' *Anthropological Theory* 7(4): 371–91.

Huizinga, Johan. 1955. *Homo Ludens: A Study of the Play Element in Culture.* Boston: Beacon Press.

Inda, Jonathan Xavier and Renato Rosaldo. 2002. 'Tracking Global Flows.' In *The Anthropology of Globalization: A Reader.* Jonathan Xavier Inda and Renato Rosaldo, eds. pp. 3–46. London: Blackwell.

Jackson, John. 2013. *Thin Description: Ethnography and the African Hebrew Israelites of Jerusalem.* Cambridge, MA: Harvard University Press.

Jacobson, Cardell K. with Lara Burton, eds. 2011. *Modern Polygamy in the United States: Historical, Legal, and Cultural Issues.* New York and Oxford: Oxford University Press.

James, William. 1902. *The Varieties of Religious Experience: A Study in Human Nature.* New York: Penguin.

Johnson, Paul Christopher. 2007. *Diaspora Conversions: Black Carib Religion and the Recovery of Africa.* Berkeley, CA: University of California Press.

——2012. Religion and Diaspora. *Advances in Research: Religion and Society* 3: 95–114.

Keane, Webb. 2002. Sincerity, 'Modernity,' and the Protestants. *Cultural Anthropology* 17(1): 65–92.

——2004. 'Language and Religion.' In *A Companion to Linguistic Anthropology.* Alessandro Duranti, ed. pp. 431–48. London: Blackwell.

——2007. *Christian Moderns: Freedom and Fetish in the Mission Encounter.* Berkeley, CA: University of California Press.

Kendall, Laurel. 2008. Of Hungry Ghosts and Other Matters of Consumption in the Republic of Korea: The Commodity Becomes a Ritual Prop. *American Ethnologist* 35(1): 154–70.

Kirsch, Thomas. 2004. Restaging the Will to Believe: Religious Pluralism, Anti-Syncretism, and the Problem of Belief. *American Anthropologist* 106(4): 699–709.

Klass, Morton. 1995. *Ordered Universes: Approaches to the Anthropology of Religion.* Boulder, CO: Westview Press.

Knibbe, Kim and Andres Droogers. 2011. Methodological Ludism and the Academic Study of Religion. *Method and Theory in the Study of Religion* 23: 283–303.

Lane, Belden C. 2001. Giving Voice to Place: Three Models for Understanding Sacred Space. *Religion and American Culture: A Journal of Interpretation* 11(1): 53–81.

Latour, Bruno. 2005. '"Thou shall not Freeze-Frame" or How not to Misunderstand the Science and Religion Debate.' In *Science, Religion, and the Human Experience*. James D. Proctor, ed. New York and Oxford: Oxford University Press.

Lawless, Elaine. 1988. *God's Peculiar People: Women's Voice and Folk Tradition in a Pentecostal Church*. Lexington, KY: University of Kentucky Press.

Lewellen, Ted C. 2002. *The Anthropology of Globalization: Cultural Anthropology Enters the 21st Century*. Westport, CT: Greenwood Press.

Lincoln, Bruce. 1994. *Authority: Construction and Corrosion*. Chicago: University of Chicago Press.

Lindholm, Charles. 1990. *Charisma*. London: Wiley-Blackwell.

——2003. Culture, Charisma, and Consciousness: The Case of the Rajneeshee. *Ethos* 30(4): 357–75.

Lofton, Kathryn. 2010. *Oprah: The Gospel of an Icon*. Berkeley, CA: University of California Press.

Luehrmann, Sonja. 2011. *Secularism Soviet Style: Teaching Atheism and Religion in a Volga Republic*. Bloomington, IN: Indiana University Press.

Mahmood, Saba. 2005. *Politics of Piety: The Islamic Revival and the Feminist Subject*. Princeton, NJ: Princeton University Press.

Makley, Charlene E. 2007. *The Violence of Liberation: Gender and Tibetan Buddhist Revival in Post-Mao China*. Berkeley, CA: University of California Press.

Malinowski, Bronislaw. 1935. *Coral Gardens and Their Magic*. New York: Dover.

——1948. *Magic, Science and Religion and Other Essays*. Long Grove, IL: Waveland Press.

Marx, Karl. 1844 [1970]. *Critique of Hegel's 'Philosophy of Right.'* Trans. Joseph O' Malley. Cambridge: Cambridge University Press.

Matthews. 1888. The Prayer of a Navajo Shaman. *American Anthropologist* 1(2): 149–71.

Mauss, Marcel. 1935 [2006]. 'Techniques of the Body.' In *Marcel Mauss: Techniques, Technology, and Civilization*. Nathan Schlanger, ed. Oxford: Berghahn.

Maxwell, David. 2007. *African Gifts of the Spirit: Pentecostalism and the Rise of a Zimbabwean Transnational Religious Movement*. Athens, OH: Ohio University Press.

McAlister, Elizabeth. 2005. Globalization and the Religious Production of Space. *Journal for the Scientific Study of Religion* 44(3): 249–55.

McBrien, Julie and Mathijs Pelkmans. 2008. Turning Marx on his Head: Missionaries, 'Extremists,' and Archaic Secularists in Post-Soviet Kyrgyzstan. *Critique of Anthropology* 28(1): 87–103.

Miles, Carrie A. 2011. '"What's Love Got to do With It?" Earthly Experience of Celestial Marriage, Past and Present.' In *Modern Polygamy in the United*

States: Political, Legal, and Cultural Issues. Cardell K. Jacobsen with Lara Burton, eds. pp. 185–208. New York and Oxford: Oxford University Press.

Monahan, Torin. 2008. Marketing the Beast: *Left Behind* and the Apocalypse Industry. *Media, Culture, and Society* 30(6): 813–30.

Murphy, Liam D. 2009. 'The Trouble with Good News: Scripture and Charisma in Northern Ireland.' In *The Social Life of Scriptures: Cross-Cultural Perspectives on Biblicism*. James S. Bielo, ed. pp. 10–29. New Brunswick, NJ: Rutgers University Press.

Needham, Rodney. 1972. *Belief, Language, and Experience*. Chicago: University of Chicago Press.

Numbers, Ronald L. 1992. *The Creationists: The Evolution of Scientific Creationism*. New York: Knopf.

O'Neill, Kevin Lewis. 2010. *City of God: Christian Citizenship in Postwar Guatemala*. Berkeley, CA: University of California Press.

Paden, William. 1988. *Religious Worlds: The Comparative Study of Religion*. Boston: Beacon Press.

Peterson, Leighton. 2013. Reel Navajo: The Linguistic Creation of Indigenous Screen Memories. *American Indian Culture and Research Journal* 35(2): 111–34.

Pouillion, Jean. 1979 [1982]. 'Remarks on the Verb "to Believe."' In *Between Belief and Transgression: Structural Essays in Religion, History, and Myth*. M. Izard and P. Smith, eds. Chicago: University of Chicago Press.

Rabinow, Paul. 1977. *Reflections on Fieldwork in Morocco*. Berkeley, CA: University of California Press.

Radin, Paul. 1937. *Primitive Religion: Its Nature and Origin*. New York: Dover. ✓

Raines, John, ed. 2002. *Marx on Religion*. Philadelphia, PA: Temple University Press.

Rappaport, Roy. 1999. *Ritual and Religion in the Making of Humanity*. Cambridge: Cambridge University Press.

Reichard, Gladys. 1944. *Prayer: The Compulsive Word*. Seattle, WA: University of Washington Press.

Robbins, Joel. 2001. God is Nothing but Talk: Modernity, Language and Prayer in a Papua New Guinea Society. *American Anthropologist* 103(4): 901–12.

——2009. Pentecostal Networks and the Spirit of Globalization: On the Social Productivity of Ritual Forms. *Social Analysis* 53(1): 55–66.

Robertson, Roland. 1992. *Globalization: Social Theory and Global Culture*. London: Sage.

Rouse, Carolyn and Janet Hoskins. 2004. Purity, Soul Food, and Sunni Islam: Explorations at the Intersection of Consumption and Resistance. *Cultural Anthropology* 19(2): 226–49.

Rudnyckyj, Daromir. 2009. Spiritual Economies: Islam and Neoliberalism in Contemporary Indonesia. *Cultural Anthropology* 24(1): 104–41.

——2010. *Spiritual Economies: Islam, Globalization, and the Afterlife of Development*. Ithaca, NY: Cornell University Press.

Ruel, Malcolm. 1982. 'Christians as Believers.' In *Religious Organizations and Religious Experiences*. J. Davis, ed. pp. 9–31. London: Academic.

Said, Edward. 1978. *Orientalism: Western Conceptions of the Orient*. New York: Penguin.

Savishinsky, Neil J. 1994. 'Transnational Popular Culture and the Global Spread of the Jamaican Rastafari Movement.' In *Across the Boundaries of Belief*. Morton Klass and Maxine K. Weisgrau, eds. pp. 347–66. Boulder, CO: Westview Press.

Schmidt, Leigh Eric. 2000. *Hearing Things: Religion, Illusion, and the American Enlightenment*. Cambridge, MA: Harvard University Press.

Scott, Eugenie. 2004. *Evolution vs. Creationism: An Introduction*. Berkeley, CA: University of California Press.

Seeman, Don. 2009. *One People, One Blood: Ethiopian-Israelis and the Return to Judaism*. New Brunswick, NJ: Rutgers University Press.

Selby, Jennifer. 2013. 'How "They" Construct "Us": Reflections on the Politics of Identity in the Field.' In *Missionary Impositions: Conversion, Resistance, and Other Challenges to Objectivity in Religious Ethnography*. pp. 41–56. Lanham, MD: Lexington Books.

Shore, Bradd. 2008. Spiritual Work, Memory Work: Revival and Recollection at Salem Camp Meeting. *Ethos* 36(1): 98–119.

Sidky, Homayun. 2009. A Shaman's Cure: The Relationship Between Altered States of Consciousness and Shamanic Healing. *Anthropology of Consciousness* 20(2): 171–97.

Sinha, Vineeta. 2011. *Religion and Commodification: 'Merchandizing' Diasporic Hinduism*. London: Routledge.

Smart, Ninian. 1973. *The Science of Religion and the Sociology of Knowledge*. Princeton, NJ: Princeton University Press.

Smith, Jonathan Z. 1998 [2004]. 'Religion, Religions, Religious.' In *Relating Religion: Essays in the Study of Religion*. Chicago: University of Chicago Press.

Spickard, James and Shawn Landres. 2002. 'Whither Ethnography? Transforming the Social-Scientific Study of Religion.' In *Personal Knowledge and Beyond: Reshaping the Ethnography of Religion*. James V. Spickard, J. Shawn Landres, and Meredith B. McGuire, eds. New York: NYU Press.

Stein, Rebecca L. and Phillip Stein. 2010. *The Anthropology of Religion, Magic, and Witchcraft*. New York: Pearson.

Steinbeck, John. 1966 [2002]. ' … like captured fireflies.' In *America and Americans*. New York: Penguin.

Stepan, Alfred. 2011. 'The Multiple Secularisms of Modern Democratic and Non-Democratic Regimes.' In *Rethinking Secularism*. Craig Calhoun, Mark

Juergensmeyer, and Jonathan van Antwerpen, eds. pp. 114–44. New York and Oxford: Oxford University Press.

Sterling, Marvin. 2010. *Babylon East: Performing Dancehall, Roots Reggae, and Rastafari in Japan*. Durham, NC: Duke University Press.

Stoller, Paul. 1984. Eye, Mind and Word in Anthropology. *L'Homme* 24(3/4): 91–114.

Stoller, Paul and Cheryl Olkes. 1987. *In Sorcery's Shadow: A Memoir of Apprenticeship among the Songhay of Niger*. Chicago: University of Chicago Press.

Subramaniam, Radhika. 1999. Culture of Suspicion: Riots and Rumor in Bombay, 1992–1993. *Transforming Anthropology* 8(1/2): 97–110.

Taylor, Charles. 2007. *A Secular Age*. Cambridge, MA: Harvard University Press.

Toumey, Christopher. 1994. *God's Own Scientists: Creationists in a Secular World*. New Brunswick, NJ: Rutgers University Press.

Turner, Edith. 1992. *Experiencing Ritual: A New Interpretation of African Healing*. Philadelphia, PA: University of Pennsylvania Press.

——1996. *The Hands Feel It: Healing and Spirit Presence among a Northern Alaskan People*. Northern Illinois University Press.

Turner, Victor. 1968. *The Drums of Affliction: A Study of Religious Processes among the Ndembu of Zambia*. Ithaca, NY: Cornell University Press.

Turner, Victor and Edith Turner. 1978. *Image and Pilgrimage in Christian Culture*. New York: Columbia University Press.

Tweed, Thomas. 1997. *Our Lady of the Exile: Diasporic Religion at a Cuban Catholic Shrine in Miami*. New York and Oxford: Oxford University Press.

——2006. *Crossing and Dwelling: A Theory of Religion*. Cambridge, MA: Harvard University Press.

Tylor, Edward. 1871. *Religion in Primitive Culture*. New York: Harper.

Urban, Hugh. 2011. *The Church of Scientology: A History of a New Religion*. Princeton, NJ: Princeton University Press.

van der Veer, Peter. 2014. *The Modern Spirit of Asia: The Spiritual and the Secular in China and India*. Princeton, NJ: Princeton University Press.

van Gennep, Arnold. 1909. *The Rites of Passage*. London: Routledge.

Waghorne, Joanne Punzo. 1999. 'The Hindu Gods in a Split-Level World: The Sri Siva-Vishnu Temple in Suburban Washington, DC.' In *Gods of the City: Religion and the American Urban Landscape*. Robert Orsi, ed. pp. 103–30. Bloomington, IN: Indiana University Press.

Wallace, Anthony F.C. 1956. Revitalization Movements. *American Anthropologist* 264–81.

——1966. *Religion: An Anthropological View*. New York: Random House.

Wanner, Catherine. 2007. *Communities of the Converted: Ukrainians and Global Evangelism*. Ithaca, NY: Cornell University Press.

Waters, W. 2001. Globalization, Socioeconomic Restructuring, and Community Health. *Journal of Community Health* 26(2): 79–92.

Watson, James. 2006. 'Transnationalism, Localization, and Fast Foods in East Asia.' In *Golden Arches East: McDonald's in East Asia*. James Watson, ed. Stanford, CA: Stanford University Press.

Weber, Max. 1905. *The Protestant Ethic and the 'Spirit' of Capitalism*. New York: Penguin.

——1922 [1978]. *Economy and Society: An Outline of Interpretive Sociology*. Berkeley, CA: University of California Press.

——1946 [1958]. *From Max Weber: Essays in Sociology*. Trans. H.H. Gerth and C. Wright Mills. New York and Oxford: Oxford University Press.

Weibel, Deana. 2013. 'Blind in a Land of Visionaries: When a Non-Pilgrim Studies Pilgrimage.' In *Missionary Impositions: Conversion, Resistance, and Other Challenges to Objectivity in Religious Ethnography*. pp. 93–108. Lanham, MD: Lexington Books.

Wiegele, Katharine. 2013. 'On Being a Participant and an Observer in Religious Ethnography: Silence, Betrayal, and Becoming.' In *Missionary Impositions: Conversion, Resistance, and Other Challenges to Objectivity in Religious Ethnography*. pp. 83–92. Lanham, MD: Lexington Books.

Wolf, Eric. 1982. *Europe and the People without History*. Berkeley, CA: University of California Press.

Yong, Amos. 2012. Observation-Participation-Subjunctivation: Methodological Play and Meaning-Making in the Study of Religion and Theology. *Religious Studies and Theology* 31(1): 17–40.

INDEX

- attend church service twice. Evaluate the definitions
of religion in Chapt 1.
- p26 activity
- Film Henry Shaman in America (ch 5)
Film May Unspeakable (ch 5)
"God's Gonna" in ch 5

CPSIA information can be obtained
at www.ICGtesting.com
Printed in the USA
FFOW01n1916301215
19795FF